D0440292

About the Author

Serafín M. Coronel-Molina is a native speaker of Quechua from the Peruvian highlands with experience in indigenous language policy and planning and second language acquisition. He has taught Spanish and Quechua at different times in various institutions in Peru, Mexico and the United States, and most recently taught both languages at the University of Michigan for two years with a joint appointment in the Department of Romance Languages and Literatures, and the Latin American and Caribbean Studies Program. He is currently finishing his doctoral program through the Graduate School of Education at the University of Pennsylvania in Philadelphia (USA). He has published scholarly articles and presented papers both nationally and internationally relating to indigenous language policy/planning in the Andean region, and Quechua sociolinguistics, including one article written entirely in Quechua about Quechua language planning, and published in the journal Amerindia: Revue d'Ethnolinguistique Amérindienne (vol. 24).

From the Author

No book comes into being without the help and support of many people, and this one is no exception. Thus I would like to gratefully acknowledge the patience and understanding of my wife, Linda Grabner-Coronel, and my daughter Flor de María, when I was so single-mindedly concentrating on the writing of this phrasebook. Even more, I owe my wife a large debt of gratitude for going so far as to stay up late with me many a night to help me proofread the text and keep details consistent throughout the book. I couldn't have done it without her eagle eyes. Annelies Mertens, my editor, is another person whose sharp eyes, linguistic knowledge and editorial skill helped polish the book into publishable form, and I thank her for her patience with my idiosyncratic working style. Finally, to my friend and native Quechua speaker Juan Arroyo, I offer my thanks for a helpful telephone conversation in and about Quechua, when he helped me to judge the comprehensibility of a few phrases I had struggled with. All of these people have contributed to making this phrasebook the useful tool it is. Grateful acknowledgment is made to Rodolfo Cerrón-Palomino/Lingüística Aymara, Lima, Peru: Centro de Estudios Regionales Andinos 'Bartolomé de Las Casas' for use of data from their Quechua language map © 2000.

From the Publisher

And the *Quechua phrasebook* relay is off ... first out of the gates is editor Annelies Mertens in fine style then senior editor Karin Vidstrup Monk who's taking the whip to Grammar and Pronunciation ... meanwhile author queries are deftly handled by editor Sophie Putman, as it comes round the corner to Sally Steward who's proofing the text and handing the dictionaries to senior editor Karina Coates. But what's this? Coming up on the inside to oversee production is acting senior editor Ben Handicott ... now editor Meg Worby's reining it in, neck and neck with star designer Patrick Marris, a real favourite in layout circles ... he's trained the promising yearling designer Yvonne Bischofberger, backed up by freelancer Jo Adams ... designer Yuki Kamimura's coming in from the outside to knock off Grammar but it's an upset folks, Grammar's winning! Beautiful form here from illustrator Rosie Silva-Guevara, will you look at the superb cover ... senior designer Fabrice Rocher's scheduled to come in on time and cartographer Natasha Velleley's handling the course as if she drew the map herself. A couple of late entries here in Karina Coates – a good finisher – and editor Emma Koch who knows her contents ... publishing manager Jim Jenkin's going to be very pleased with backing this one. What a magnificent result folks and a great end to the season!

CONTENTS

6   Contents

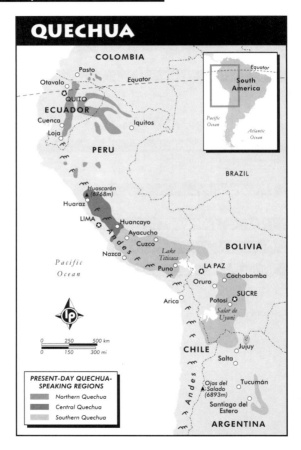

QUECHUA

COLOMBIA

Pasto

Otavalo

QUITO

ECUADOR

Cuenca

Loja

Equator

Iquitos

PERU

BRAZIL

Huascarán
(6768m)

Huaraz

LIMA

Huancayo

Ayacucho

Cuzco

Nazca

Lake
Titicaca

Puno

BOLIVIA

LA PAZ

Oruro

Cochabamba

SUCRE

Potosí

Arica

Salar de
Uyuni

*Pacific
Ocean*

Andes

CHILE

Jujuy

Salta

Ojas del
Salado
(6893m)

Tucumán

Santiago del
Estero

ARGENTINA

Equator

South
America

*Pacific
Ocean*

*Atlantic
Ocean*

0   250   500 km
0   150   300 mi

**PRESENT-DAY QUECHUA-
SPEAKING REGIONS**

Northern Quechua

Central Quechua

Southern Quechua

INTRODUCTION

Travelling in the Andes will be much more enjoyable and worthwhile if you can speak some Quechua, the language of the Incas, also known as *runasimi*, roo·nah·*see*·mee.

Despite the official status of Spanish, which was brought to Latin America by the conquistadors, you'll find that Quechua is spoken in six South American countries: Peru, Bolivia, Ecuador, Colombia, Argentina and Chile. Most Quechua speakers are found in the Andes, although some live in the jungle or on the coast.

Quechua is actually a family of languages that has been spoken by many different peoples in the Andean region long before the Incas began to consolidate their empire in the 13th century AD. The Inca empire reached the height of its development in the 15th century, just 70 years before the arrival of the Spaniards in 1532. The Incas adopted Quechua as their official language in order to facilitate communication with their multilingual subjects.

Today, there are approximately 24 different dialects of Quechua, divided into regional branches known as Northern, Central and Southern Quechua. All these varieties combined are spoken by approximately eight to 10 million people, making Quechua the most widely spoken indigenous language in the Americas.

IN CASE I DON'T SEE YOU ...

The expressions *Wuynus diyas*, *Wuynas tardis* and *Wuynas nuchis*, for 'Good morning', 'Good afternoon' and 'Good evening/night', were borrowed long ago from Spanish and have become much more common than the original Quechua words.

INTRODUCTION

In this phrasebook, we use the Cuzco variety of Quechua, a southern Peruvian dialect (in the Southern Quechua linguistic branch), which is the most widely spoken in the Quechua family. It's well understood in the Peruvian departments of Apurímac, Ayacucho, Cuzco, Huancavelica and Puno, in all of Bolivia, and in the province of Santiago del Estero in Argentina, despite small differences. It can be partially understood in all other Quechua-speaking areas of the Andes, although there are some minor regional variations in pronunciation, word endings and vocabulary. You should be able to get your basic message across with Cuzco Quechua wherever you travel in the Andes.

By speaking some Quechua, you'll break down invisible barriers and show people that you have a genuine interest in their culture and language. Hearing it spoken by foreigners, however haltingly, will be appreciated by native speakers. They'll gain through seeing their language valued by visitors, and your experience will be enhanced through the goodwill shared with them.

ABBREVIATIONS USED IN THIS BOOK

adj	adjective	pl	plural
adv	adverb	prep	preposition
f	feminine	pron	pronoun
inf	infinitive	sg	singular
m	masculine	v	verb
n	noun		

PRONUNCIATION

Quechua is fairly straightforward to pronounce. Beside each word and phrase in this book, you'll find a simple pronunciation guide. It appears in colour and words are divided into syllables with a dot. The Quechua writing system is represented by italic letters.

VOWEL SOUNDS

In spoken Quechua, there are five vowel sounds that correspond to the three basic written vowels *(a, i* and *u)* of the official Quechua writing system, as approved by the Peruvian government in 1985.

Sound	Description	Quechua	
ah	as the 'a' in 'father'	*a*	
ee	as the 'ee' in 'see'	*i, iy*	
e	as the 'e' in 'bet'	*i*	(when found before or after consonants *q, q'* or *qh*)
oo	as the 'oo' in 'hoot'	*u, uw*	
o	as the 'o' in 'got'	*u*	(when found before or after consonants *q, q'* or *qh*)

PRONUNCIATION

Diphthongs

The Quechua writing system combines the letters *w* and *y* with *a*, *i* or *u* to form the following diphthongs (vowel sounds).

Sound	Description	Quechua
ow	as the 'ow' in 'vow'	*aw*
ai	as the 'ai' in 'aisle'	*ay*
yoo	as the 'u' in 'union'	*iw*
ay	as the 'ay' in 'day'	*ay* (when before or after the consonants *q*, *q'* or *qh*)
ui	as the 'ouie' in 'Louie'	*uy*
oy	as the 'oy' in 'toy'	*uy* (when before or after the consonants *q*, *q'* or *qh*)

CONSONANT SOUNDS

Most consonants are pronounced basically as they are in English. A few of the sounds are not common in English, but they shouldn't prove too difficult – the most challenging might be the 'ejective' consonants, explained on page 14.

SAY IT WITH PRIDE

According to some researchers, the term *runasimi*, roo·nah·*see*·mee, which means 'human speech', was used pejoratively by Spaniards in colonial times to distinguish 'Indian speech' from *kastillasimi*, kah·stee·lyah·*see*·mee, 'Castilian speech'. Nowadays, this term has lost these connotations and is used with pride by Quechua speakers as a name for their language.

Sound	Description	Quechua
ch	as the 'ch' in 'chew'	ch
f	as the 'f' in 'fun'	ph
g	as the 'g' in 'gun'	g
h	as the 'h' in 'hope'	h
k	as the 'k' in 'skill'	k, q
kh	as the 'ch' in the Scottish *loch*	k, q, p (at the end of a word)
l	as the 'l' in 'land'	l
ly	as the 'lli' in 'billion' with the middle of the tongue against the roof of the mouth	ll
m	as the 'm' in 'much'	m
n	as the 'n' in 'note'	n
ny	as the 'ny' in 'canyon'	ñ
p	as the 'p' in 'spot'	p
r	like a very short 'd' sound, not like an English 'r'	r
rr	a trilled 'r'	rr
s	as the 's' in 'saw'	s
sh	as the 'sh' in 'short'	sh
t	as the 't' in 'stop'	t
w	as the 'w' in 'wig'	w
y	as the 'y' in 'yes'	y

PRONUNCIATION

Aspiration & Ejectives

Aspiration refers to consonants which are pronounced with a small puff of air, as the initial 'p' in the English 'pot' (as opposed to the 'p' in 'spot' – hold your hand in front of your mouth when you say the two words and feel the difference). The meaning of a word can change depending on whether or not a consonant is aspirated. See the box on page 16 for examples of this. In our pronunciation guide, aspiration is indicated with the addition of -h. In written Quechua, aspirated consonants are indicated by the letter *h* after the initial consonant.

Symbol	Sound	Letter
ch-h	as the 'ch-h' in 'Dutch hope'	*chh*
k-h	as the 'k-h' in 'duck house'	*kh, qh*
p-h	in the Cuzco area, this sound is similar to an English 'f'; in other areas, the sound is closer to a very soft, breathy 'p'	*ph*
t-h	as the 't-h' in 'hot house'	*th*

Ejectives are consonants which are pronounced by stopping the airflow momentarily at the back of the throat and then releasing it. This is similar to the 'tt' in the cockney 'bottle', although other parts of the mouth (the lips, for example) can be used in conjunction with this throat movement to create the ejective sounds which occur in Quechua. Like aspiration, the use of ejective consonants can change the meaning of a word (see the box on page 16). In our pronunciation guide, an ejective is indicated with an apostrophe (') following the initial consonant sound.

Symbol	Sound	Letter
ch'	sharper and more abrupt than the 'ch' in 'chew'	ch'
k'	made with a click at the back of the throat	k'
p'	made by briefly closing the lips, and then 'popping' or unsticking the lips	p'
q'	made with a click in the throat like the ejective k', but strongly, at the very back of the throat	q'
t'	made with a sharp clicking of the tip of the tongue, a bit like the 'tt' in American English 'button', but more exaggerated	t'

PRONUNCIATION

STRESS

Words are generally stressed on the second last syllable. A stressed syllable in this book is indicated by the use of italics:

| *paqarichiy* | pah·kah·*ree*·chee | to give life/ to establish |

If the word only has two syllables, then it will be the first syllable that's stressed:

| *pallay* | *pah*·lyai | to gather |

An exception to this pattern occurs when an accent is marked over a vowel, indicating that the stress falls on that syllable:

| ¡achakáw! | ah·chah·*kow!* | Ouch! That's hot! |
| arí | ah·*ree* | yes |

PRONUNCIATION

IT'S A BLOW OUT

The pronunciation of aspirated and ejective consonants is one of the defining characteristics of the Cuzco, Puno and Bolivian varieties of Quechua. Be aware that these sounds alter the meaning of words, as these examples show:

chaki	chah·kee	foot/leg
ch'aki	ch'ah·kee	dry
tanta	tahn·tah	gathered together
t'anta	t'ahn·tah	bread
thanta	t-hahn·tah	old/used/worn out

If you find it difficult to make these distinctions at first, keep trying and it will come. Don't worry too much if you do make a mistake though – your meaning will often be clear from the context.

INTONATION

Intonation patterns in Quechua vary from those of English in one very important way – questions have the same intonation as statements (in Quechua, essentially a falling one). Instead of a rising intonation, specific question words or prefixes indicate that a question is being asked. Quechua also uses a different way of expressing exclamation – the intonation doesn't actually change, instead there is an increased stress on the syllable that emphasises the statement.

GRAMMAR

This chapter is one of the few overviews of Quechua grammar you'll see. It's not exhaustive, but it will give you enough of a foundation to understand the basic structure of the language so you can construct simple sentences of your own.

In Quechua, sentences are built around basic root words, and the rest of the meaning is added to the sentence by attaching suffixes. In this chapter, to make it easier to distinguish root words from their suffixes, we have used a hyphen between the root and each suffix. The root word always comes first.

There are no irregular verbs in Quechua – all Quechua verbs follow the rules according to each tense. The tenses presented in this phrasebook are the most essential ones.

The following abbreviations are used in this chapter:

adj	adjective	n	noun
assert	assertive	neg	negative
emph	emphatic	obj	object
excl	exclusive 'we'	obl	obligation
fut	future tense	past	past tense
imp	imperative	poss	possessive
incl	inclusive 'we'	pres	present tense
int	interrogative	top	topic
interj	interjection/	uncert	uncertainty
	exclamation	v	verb
lit	literal translation		

WORD ORDER

In general, the basic sentence word order in Quechua is subject-object-verb:

Satuku is eating bread.   *Satuku t'anta-ta-n mikhu-sha-n.*
                          (lit: Satuku bread-obj-assert eat-ing-is)

Note that the assertive suffix indicates that the speaker is stating something from personal experience. See the full explanation on page 22.

Because of the nature of a suffix-based system, word order is quite flexible. You can put any word first to emphasise it:

Satuku is eating *bread*.   *T'anta-ta-n Satuku mikhu-sha-n.*
                            (lit: bread-obj-assert Satuku eat-ing-is)

Here it's 'bread' that's emphasised.

ARTICLES

There's no word for 'the', but 'a/an' is *huq* (literally 'one'). It can also mean 'some' when used with a plural noun:

a restaurant   *huq mikhuna wasi*   (lit: one food house)

some people   *huq runa-kuna*   (lit: one person-pl)

ROOT WORDS

Root words are the building blocks of a sentence, onto which suffixes are attached to create the full meaning.

SUFFIXES

Suffixes do the functional work in a sentence, showing how the various root words work together to give meaning. For instance, *wasi*, 'house', is a noun, but by adding the suffixes *-cha* (which changes certain nouns to verbs) and *-y* (which marks the infinitive), it becomes the verb *wasi-cha-y*, 'to build (a house)'.

Dependent Suffixes

Dependent suffixes can only be used with certain parts of speech or parts of a sentence: they add meaning to a word. An example in English would be the prefix 'un-', as in 'unusual': it cannot be used on its own, but when combined with other words, it carries a distinct meaning (it creates the oposite of the word).

There are three major groups of dependent suffixes:

1. The **nominals** are used only with nouns and pronouns and include the subject marker, object marker, number markers, possessives and several prepositions.

2. The **verbals** are used only with verbs. These include tense, mood and command markers. See Verb page 32.

3. The **derivational suffixes** change one part of speech to another. They have a parallel in English: eg, by adding '-ness', the adjective 'sad' can be turned into the noun 'sadness'. Each specific derivational suffix can only be attached to a specific part of speech, eg, the suffix *-sqa* can only be added to a verb to form an adjective, never to form a noun (see the table below).

GRAMMAR

to get tired (v)	*sayk'u-y*	tired (adj)	*sayk'u-sqa*
to sit down (v)	*tiya-y*	seat; place to sit (n)	*tiya-na*
head (n)	*uma*	big-headed (adj)	*uma-sapa*
stone (n)	*rumi*	to change to stone (v)	*rumi-ya-y*
little (adj)	*pisi*	scarcity (n)	*pisi-y*
hot (adj)	*rupha*	to burn (v)	*rupha-chi-y*

Here are some examples of nominal dependent suffixes, and their uses:

because of/due to/ on behalf of	-rayku
I came to Cuzco because of the Inti Raymi Festival.	*Inti Raymi-rayku-n Qusqu-man hamurqa-ni.* (lit: Inti Raymi-because_ of-assert Cuzco-to came-I)

for (the purpose of)	-paq
I work for my family.	*Ayllu-y-paq llank'a-ni.* (lit: family-my-for work-I)

from	-manta
She/He is returning from Potosí.	*Putusi llaqta-manta kutimu-sha-n.* (lit: Potosí city-from return-ing-she/he)

in (location)	-pi
I work in Chinchero.	*Chinchiru-pi llank'a-ni.* (lit: Chinchero-in work-I)

possessive ('s)	-q/-pa (after vowel/consonant)
man's	*qhari-q* (lit: man-of)

until	-kama
The road goes to Machu Picchu.	*Machu Pikchu-kama ñan ri-sha-n.* (lit: Machu Picchu-until road go-ing-it)

with	-wan
They're talking with the police.	*Wardiya-wan rima-sha-nku.* (lit: police-with talk-ing-they)

MULTI-FUNCTION SUFFIXES: -TA & -MAN

The suffix *-ta* is can serve numerous functions within a sentence, including:

- object marker, direct and indirect

  I see him.   *Pay-ta qhawa-ni.*
                        (lit: he-obj see-I)

  Can you help me   *¿Yanapa-wanki-man-chu qipiy-ta*
    find my backpack?   *maskhay-ta?*
                        (lit: help-me-could-int
                           backpack-obj look_for-obj)

Note that as an indirect object *-ta* can only be used with verbs that don't involve movement of the direct object (see second example). The two verbs – help and find – don't involve movement of the direct object 'backpack'.

- destination, meaning 'to(wards)'

  I'm going to Apurimac. *Apurimaq-ta ri-sha-ni.*
                          (lit: Apurimac-to go-ing-I)

- derivational suffix, changing adjectives to adverbs

  good   *allin*

  He does well.   *Allin-ta ruwa-n.*
                          (lit: good-adv do-he)

Here, the two functions of object marker and destination come together in one sentence:

  I want to go   *Apurimaq-ta riy-ta muna-ni.*
    to Apurimac.   (lit: Apurimac-to go-obj want-I)

continues on next page

MULTI-FUNCTION SUFFIXES: -TA & -MAN

continues from previous page

The suffix *-man* is similar to *-ta* in that it serves as both an object and destination marker (also meaning 'to(wards)'). Its function as object marker, however, is limited to indirect objects only. It's applied in cases where verbs involving movement are used, and in connection with a concrete noun or the pronoun *pay*.

I give him money.	*Qulqi-ta pay-man qu-ni.* (lit: money-obj he-obj give-I)
to/towards	*-man*
This bus is going to Ecuador.	*Ikwadur suyu-man kay uniwus ri-sha-n.* (lit: Ecuador region-to this bus go-ing-it)

Independent Suffixes

The use of independent suffixes is not limited to a particular part of speech. These are attached to the key word in the sentence (which can be any part of speech) but express the speaker's attitude to the whole sentence.

Assertion

The suffix *-n/-mi* (after vowel/consonant respectively) indicates that the speaker is stating something from personal experience.

I speak English.	*Nuqa inlis-ta-n rima-ni.* (lit: I English-obj-assert speak-I)
My stomach hurts.	*Wiksa-y-mi nana-wa-sha-n.* (lit: stomach-my-assert hurt-to_me-ing-it)

Hearsay

The suffix *-s/-si* (after vowel/consonant respectively) indicates that the speaker knows the information second-hand.

People say that village is far away.	*Chay llaqta sinchi karu-s.* (lit: that village very far-hearsay)
People say that she/he speaks Quechua.	*Pay-si runasimi-ta rima-n.* (lit: she/he-hearsay Quechua-obj speak-she/he)

Uncertainty

The suffix *-ch/-cha* (after vowel/consonant) indicates uncertainty over the veracity or validity of words.

He probably speaks Quechua.	*Pay-cha runasimi-ta rima-n.* (lit: he-uncert Quechua-obj speak-he)
There are probably sandals in that store.	*Chay tinda-pi-ch usut'a-kuna ka-n.* (lit: that store-in-uncert sandal-pl there_is-it)

Topic Marker

The suffix *-qa* is an important independent suffix because it marks the repetition of the topic – or main idea or subject – in the conversation. It's therefore referred to as a topic marker.

You don't need to use this suffix the first time you mention a specific subject in a conversation, but after that you must add it to the end of that subject (after all other suffixes, if any exist):

Your brother is sick.	*Turay-ki unqu-shan-mi.*
He can't go to Quito.	*Manan pay-qa Kitu-ta riy-ta ati-n-chu.* (lit: brother-your sick-is-assert. no he-top Quito-obj go-to can-he-neg)

Emphasis

The emphatic suffix **-má** is used to express surprise, to correct someone else's statement, to correct oneself, or to simply emphasise a point. It's always the final suffix to be added to a word, and is stressed:

> He came all the way
> from Cochabamba!
>
> *¡Quchapampa-manta-má*
> *kuti-rqa-mu-n!*
> (lit: Cochabamba-from-emph
>   come_back-past-to_here-he!)

Others

Other important independent suffixes are **-chu**, used to mark questions or negatives (see Questions on page 39), **-pis/-pas**, meaning 'and/also/too' (see Conjunctions on page 42) and **-ña**, meaning 'already'.

> I already did it.
>
> *Tuku-rqu-ni-ña-n.*
> (lit: finish-just-I-already-assert)

NOUNS

Nouns are root words (see Root Words, page 18). In general, a noun is expressed as a simple singular entity. If you want to make it plural or modify it in any other way, you do so through the use of specific suffixes.

WE X TWO

It's important to note that, unlike English, Quechua has two categories of the first person plural (we/us). The inclusive category includes the speaker, the listener and anyone else to whom the speaker is referring ('you, me and everyone'). The exclusive category includes the speaker and anyone else to whom she or he is referring, but not the listener ('me and the others, but not you').

Plurals

To make plural nouns, simply add the suffix *-kuna*. Note, however, that if a specific number or quantity of something is mentioned, the plural suffix does not need to be added. (See Numbers, page 167, for more on this.)

store	*tinda*
stores	*tinda-**kuna*** (lit: store-pl)
one boat	*huq wampu* (lit: one boat)
ten boats	*chunka wampu* (lit: ten boat)

Gender

Quechua does not express gender for inanimate objects, only for animals and people. To indicate gender for people, use *warmi*, 'woman', or *qhari*, 'man'. If the gender of an animal is relevant, you have to specifically identify it as *china*, 'female', or *urqu*, 'male'. So a 'female dog' would be *china alqu* and a 'male dog' *urqu alqu*.

Some words borrowed from Spanish explicitly indicate gender, such as *awilu*, 'grandfather', and *awila*, 'grandmother'.

PRONOUNS
Subject Pronouns

Subject pronouns can be expressed with individual words as well as with suffixes. If the context of a sentence makes clear who or what the subject is, the pronoun is not required. The suffixes often provide all the information necessary. These are the individual subject pronouns:

SINGULAR		PLURAL	
I	*nuqa*	we (incl)	*nuqanchis*
		we (excl)	*nuqayku*
you (sg)	*qan*	you (pl)	*qankuna*
she/he	*pay*	they	*paykuna*

GRAMMAR

Subject/Object Pronoun Suffixes

As with just about everything else in Quechua, personal pronouns are expressed through the use of suffixes which identify both the subject and object in a sentence. These suffixes, however, are attached to the verb and are compulsory in the sentence. The pronoun suffixes change depending on verb tense.

I give you money.   *Nuqa qulqi-ta qu-**yki**.*
(lit: I money-obj give-I_
to_ you_sg_obj_pres)

Suffixes for Present Tense

Singular

Subject \ Object	me	you	her/him
I	-	-yki	-
you	-wanki	-	-
she/he	-wan	-sunki	-
we (incl)	-	-	-
we (excl)	-	-ykiku	-
you	-wankichis	-	-
they	-wanku	-sunkiku	-

Plural

Subject \ Object	us (incl)	us (excl)	you	them
I	-	-	-ykichis	-
you	-	-wankiku	-	-
she/he	-wanchis	-wanku	-sunkichis	-
we (incl)	-	-	-	-
we (excl)	-	-	-ykiku	-
you	-	-wankiku	-	-
they	-wanchis	-wanku	-sunkichis	-

GRAMMAR

There's a different suffix for each subject/object combination and for each tense of the verb. Here, the suffix *-yki* indicates the subject, object and tense of the verb at the one time.

I give you (sg) beer.   *Aha-ta qu-yki.*
(lit: beer-obj give-I_to_
you_sg_obj_pres)

The following tables show possible subject/object combinations. Some subject/object pronoun combinations are not logically possible in Quechua, so are indicated by empty cells.

Suffixes for Past Tense

Singular

Subject \ Object	me	you	her/him
I	-	-rqayki	-
you	-warqanki	-	-
she/he	-warqan	-rqasunki	-
we (incl)	-	-	-
we (excl)	-	-rqaykiku	-
you	-warqankichis	-	-
they	-warqanku	-rqasunkiku	-

Plural

Subject \ Object	us (incl)	us (excl)	you	them
I	-	-	-rqaykichis	-
you	-	-warqankiku	-	-
she/he	-warqanchis	-warqanku	-rqasunkichis	-
we (incl)	-	-	-	-
we (excl)	-	-	-rqaykiku	-
you	-	-warqankiku	-	-
they	-warqanchis	-warqanku	-rqasunkichis	-

GRAMMAR

Note that for the third person (sg/pl) there are no specific object pronoun suffixes. Instead, you'd use the subject pronoun **pay(kuna)** (see page 25) plus the indirect object marker **-man** to express the object 'to him/her/them'. You then add the appropriate subject pronoun suffix to the verb (**-ni** in the example):

Suffixes for Future Tense

Singular

Object \ Subject	me	you	her/him
I	-	-sayki	-
you	-wanki	-	-
she/he	-wanqa	-sunki	-
we (incl)	-	-	-
we (excl)	-	-saykiku	-
you	-wankichis	-	-
they	-wanqaku	-sunkiku	-

Plural

Object \ Subject	us (incl)	us (excl)	you	them
I	-	-	-saykichis	-
you	-	-wankiku	-	-
she/he	-wasunchis	-wanqaku	-sunkichis	-
we (incl)	-	-	-	-
we (excl)	-	-	-saykiku	-
you	-	-wankiku	-	-
they	-wasunchis	-wanqaku	-sunkichis	-

I give them sweets.

Nuqa misk'i-ta
paykuna-man *qu-ni.*
(lit: I sweet-obj them-obj
give-I)

GRAMMAR

ADJECTIVES

Adjectives come before nouns. Only the nouns are pluralised, not the adjectives.

beautiful day	*sumaq p'unchay*	(lit: pretty day)
black donkeys	*yana asnu-kuna*	(lit: black donkey-pl)

Kusi is buying some beautiful clothes.	*Kusi sumaq p'achakuna-ta ranti-sha-n.*	
	(lit: Kusi beautiful clothes-obj buy-ing-he)	

The concept of 'very' can be indicated by repeating the adjective, as in:

very far away	*karu karu*	(lit: far far)
very big	*hatun hatun*	(lit: big big)

GRAMMAR

Comparatives

In Quechua, *aswan*, 'more', and *pisi*, 'less', are placed in front of the adjective to make a comparison:

big	*hatun*	
bigger	*aswan hatun*	(lit: more big)
smaller	*pisi hatun*	(lit: less big)

It's also very common for either the emphatic suffix *-má* (see page 24) or the assertive suffix *-n/-mi* to be added to the end of the adjective as well:

I'm younger than him.	*Pay-manta aswan wayna-má ka-ni.*
	(lit: she/he-from more young-emph am-I)

Superlatives

The superlative is expressed using 'the most', **lliw-manta aswan ...-n/-mi**, or 'the least', **lliw-manta aswan pisi ...-n/-mi**. The blank is filled in by an adjective:

This town is the biggest.	*Kay llaqta-qa **lliw-manta aswan** hatun-mi.* (lit: this town-top all-from more big-assert)
That town is the smallest.	*Chay llaqta-qa **lliw-manta aswan pisi** hatun-mi.* (lit: that town-top all-from more less big-assert)

ADVERBS

Adverbs can be either words derived from adjectives through the use of the adverb marker **-ta** (like adding '-ly' in English), or independent root words. Here are some common adverbs:

easily	*chhalla-lla/phasil-cha-lla*
in this way/manner	*hina*
quickly/rapidly	*usqhay(-lla)*
slowly/carefully	*alli-lla-manta*
very	*ancha/sinchi/nishu*
well	*allin-ta/kusa*

All of the above are 'stand-alone' root words, although some of them carry suffixes to make them adverbs.

DEMONSTRATIVES

In Quechua, words like 'this', 'that', 'these' and 'those' can be adjectives when describing a noun, as in *kay qhatu*, 'this market', or pronouns when replacing a noun if it has already been mentioned:

This town is lovely,   ***Kay*** *llaqta sumaq-mi,*
    that one is not.   *chay-qa manan sumaq-chu.*
       (lit: this town beautiful-assert,
         that-top not beautiful-neg)

There's no difference between singular and plural demonstrative adjectives in Quechua, since it's the noun and not the adjective that is pluralised. Demonstrative pronouns add the suffix *-kuna* to pluralise: eg, *kay-kuna,* literally 'this-plural', thus 'these'.

However, a distinction is made between three – rather than only two – degrees of distance:

this/these	*kay/ankay*
that/those (closer to listener)	*chay/anchay*
that/those (further away from listener and speaker)	*chaqay/chhaqay/haqay*

The second form of 'that/those' does not really have an equivalent in English.

This boat is going   ***Kay*** *wampu-qa*
    to Puno.   *Punu-man-mi ri-sha-n.*
       (lit: this boat-top
         Puno-to-assert go-ing-it)

Those boats over there   ***Chaqay*** *wampu-kuna*
    are small.   *huch'uy-mi.*
       (lit: that boat-pl small-assert)

GRAMMAR

A BEAUTIFUL DESIRE TO LOVE

Muna-y is a very versatile word, meaning 'to like,' as well as 'to love', 'to desire'; 'to want' and 'to need'. As an adjective, it can mean 'good', 'beautiful' or 'lovely', and as a noun, 'desire' 'love' or 'goodwill'.

POSSESSIVES

Possession in Quechua is shown by adding a possessive suffix to the noun being possessed. You can also add a possessive pronoun when you want to clarify the possession. The possessive pronouns consist of subject pronouns with the suffixes *-q* and *-pa* added (after vowel/consonant). The suffixes are the essential elements for showing possession and are added to the nouns right after the root word, whereas possessive pronouns are mostly used for emphasis.

I just found my backpack.	*Qipi-y-ta tari-rqu-ni-n.* (lit: backpack-my-obj find-just-I-assert)
These skirts are ours.	*Nuqanchis-pa-n kay pullira-kuna-qa.* (lit: ours-assert this skirt-pl-top)

VERBS

Verbs will always have at least one suffix. This obligatory suffix will show what tense (past, present or future) the verb is in, and who or what the subject of the verb is, ie first, second or third person, singular or plural. The suffix *-y* indicates the infinitive of the verb, eg, *ka-y*, 'to be', and this form is used in the dictionaries.

Possessive Pronoun		Possessive Suffix	
nuqa-q	mine	*-y*	my
qan-pa	yours (sg)	*-yki*	your (sg)
pay-pa	hers/his	*-n*	her/his
nuqanchis-pa	ours (incl)	*-nchis*	our (incl)
nuqayku-q	ours (excl)	*-yku*	our (excl)
qankuna-q	yours (pl)	*-ykichis*	your (pl)
paykuna-q	theirs	*-nku*	their

Present Tense

The present tense is used either to indicate an action that occurs once in the present, or to indicate habitual actions. To form it, simply add the appropriate subject pronoun suffix (see Pronoun Suffixes page 26) to the verb root.

Remember that the subject pronoun suffix is essential, but the subject pronoun in parentheses is optional.

I speak Quechua.   *Nuqa runasimi-ta rima-ni.*
              (lit: I Quechua-obj speak-I)

Person	Subject Pronoun	Object ('Quechua')	Obj Suffix	Verb Root ('to speak')	Subject Pron Suffix
I	*(Nuqa)*	*runasimi*	*-ta*	*rima*	*-ni*
you (sg)	*(Qan)*				*-nki*
she/he	*(Pay)*				*-n*
we (incl)	*(Nuqanchis)*				*-nchis*
we (excl)	*(Nuqayku)*				*-yku*
you (pl)	*(Qankuna)*				*-nkichis*
they	*(Paykuna)*				*-nku*

To express an action that's in the process of happening (like the '-ing' form in English), insert the suffix *-sha* between the verb root and the subject pronoun suffix:

She's/He's speaking   *Pay runasimi-ta rima-sha-n.*
   Quechua.   (lit: she/he Quechua-obj
                 speak-ing-she/he_pres)

Past Tense

To form the past tense, add the suffix *-rqa* in front of the subject pronoun suffix. Note that in the past tense, the suffix *-n* for the third person singular is optional.

Person	Subject Pronoun	Object ('Quechua')	Obj Suffix	Verb Root ('to speak')	Past Suffix	Subject Pron Suffix
I	*(Nuqa)*	*inlis*	*-ta*	*rima*	*-rqa*	*-ni*
you (sg)	*(Qan)*					*-nki*
she/he	*(Pay)*					*(-n)*
we (incl)	*(Nuqanchis)*					*-nchis*
we (excl)	*(Nuqayku)*					*-yku*
you (pl)	*(Qankuna)*					*-nkichis*
they (pl)	*(Paykuna)*					*-nku*

She/He spoke English.   *Pay inlis-ta rima-**rqa**-(n).*
(lit: she/he English-obj speak-past-(she/he_pres))

Future Tense

The future tense is used primarily to express simple future actions ('I'll come tomorrow.'/'Will you come tomorrow?') and probability when used with the 'uncertainty' validator *-ch/-cha* (after vowel/consonant).

In the future tense, most subject pronoun suffixes change form rather than adding yet another suffix to show the tense. Two subject pronoun suffixes, however, remain the same as in the present tense: the singular and plural forms of 'you', *-nki* (sg) and *-nkichis* (pl). When these appear, you'll need to judge by the context whether the speaker refers to the present or the future.

I'll speak Spanish.   *Nuqa kastillanu-ta rima-**saq**.*
(lit: I Spanish-obj speak-I_fut)

Person	Subject Pronoun	Object ('Spanish')	Obj Suffix	Verb Root ('to speak')	Subject Pron Suffix & Future Tense
I	*(Nuqa)*				-saq
you (sg)	*(Qan)*				-nki
she/he	*(Pay)*	kastillanu	-ta	rima	-nqa
we (incl)	*(Nuqanchis)*				-sunchis
we (excl)	*(Nuqayku)*				-saqku
you (pl)	*(Qankuna)*				-nkichis
they	*(Paykuna)*				-nqaku

They will speak Spanish.   *Paykuna kastillanu-ta rima-nqaku.*
(lit: they Spanish-obj speak-they_fut)

Imperative

The imperative is a direct command which tells your listener to do something. This is indicated by the suffix *-y*:

Come here!   *¡Hamu-y!*
(lit: come-imp)

In the case of a negative command, the sentence begins with *ama* and the suffix *-chu* is added to the verb as the last suffix:

Don't do that!   *¡Ama chay-ta ruwa-y-chu!*
(lit: don't that-obj do-imp-neg)

(See also Modals, page 37.)

To Be

The verb *ka-y* means 'to be', in the sense of 'to exist', and is also used to describe something or someone, as in *Nuqa turista-n ka-ni*, 'I'm a tourist' (lit: I tourist-assert am-I). *Ka-y* can also mean 'there is/are' when stating something.

Don't confuse the verb *ka-y*, with the demonstrative adjective *kay*, 'this', which has the same spelling (see Demonstratives page 31).

You (sg) are a pretty girl.	*Qan sumaq warma-cha-n ka-nki.* (lit: you-sg beautiful girl-little-assert are-you)
She's/He's on the train.	*Pay trin-pi-n ka-sha-n.* (lit: she/he train-in-assert be-ing-she/he)
We (incl) are tired.	*Nuqanchis sayk'usqa-n ka-nchis.* (lit: we incl tired-assert are-we_incl)
They're in Coricancha.	*Paykuna Qurikancha-pi-n ka-sha-nku.* (lit: they Coricancha-in-assert be-ing-they)
There are a lot of mountains around this town.	*Kay llaqta-pi askha urqu-kuna-n ka-nku.* (lit: this town-in many mountain-pl-assert are-they)

Note that when defining someone or something in the third person, you don't use the verb *ka-y* (or any other verb):

She's/He's a foreigner.	*Pay hawa runa-n.* (lit: she/he outside_ person-assert)
They're healers.	*Paykuna hampiq-mi.* (lit: they healer-assert)

To Have

The verb **ka-y**, 'to be', also serves the function of the English 'to have' in the sense of possession. Literally, it points out something that is or isn't in someone's possession:

Do you have children? ¿**Ka-n-chu** wawa-yki?
(lit: there_is-she/he-int
child-your)

Yes, I do. Arí, **ka-n-mi**.
(lit: yes there_is-she/he-assert)

No, I don't. Mana-n **ka-n-chu**.
(lit: no-assert there_is-she/
he-neg)

I have a house. Wasi-yuq-mi **ka-ni**.
(lit: house-with-assert am-I)

MODALS

Modals modify the meaning of other verbs in a sentence. They express ability, necessity, desire or need, as in 'can read', 'need to go' and 'want to drink'. As you'd expect, modals also take the form of suffixes.

Must; Should

The simple suffix **-na** plus the appropriate possessive suffix (see Possessives page 32) added to the verb, in that order, indicates the notion of 'must' in Quechua. You can also use the verb **ka-y**, 'to have', which is used only when the obligation implied is unavoidable ('have to') – in which case the progressive form of the present tense **ka-sha-n** (see page 33) is recommended. When the obligation implied is avoidable (eg, 'should' or 'ought to'), the verb **ka-y** is not used.

Must; Have To; Need To

I have to work. Llank'a-**na**-y ka-sha-n.
(lit: work-obl-my be-ing-it)

We (excl) have to leave. Lluqsi-**na**-yku ka-sha-n.
(lit: leave-obl-our be-ing-it)

Ought To; Should

I should eat.

*Mikhu-**na-y**.*
(lit: eat-obl-my)

We (incl) ought to rest.

*Sama-**na-nchis**.*
(lit: rest-obl-our_incl)

Can; To be Able

The verb ***ati-y*** meaning 'to be able/to have the ability' is used in a similar way as its English counterpart:

They can dance.

*Paykuna tusu-y-ta **ati**-nku.*
(lit: they dance-inf-obj can-
they_pres)

Must Not; Cannot

Use the negative command form (see Imperatives, page 35). Quechua speakers would typically just say ***Ama chay unu-ta ukyay-chu***, 'Don't drink that water' (lit: don't that water-obj drink-neg).

Like

Muna-y is the verb for 'to like' in Quechua. It can be used by itself or with another verb:

I like Cuzco.

*Nuqa Qusqu-ta **muna**-ni.*
(lit: I Cuzco-obj like-I)

We (excl) like to
buy clothes.

*Nuqayku p'acha-ta
ranti-y-ta **muna**-yku.*
(lit: we clothes-obj
buy-inf-obj like-we_excl)

QUESTIONS
'Yes/No' Questions

To ask a 'yes/no' question, add the independent suffix *-chu* to the most relevant word in the question. Note that the question marker is on the verb:

Are you (sg) married?	*¿Kasaru-**chu** ka-nki?* (lit: married-int are-you_sg)

The suffix can also be attached to the noun (or to adjectives or adverbs if those are the elements being questioned):

Are you going to Cochabamba?	*¿Quchapampa-ta-**chu*** *ri-sha-nki?* (lit: Cochabamba-obj-int go-ing-you)

You can answer 'yes/no' questions either with *arí*, 'yes', or *mana*, 'no'. If, in an affirmative answer, you repeat the entire question, the assertive suffix *-n/-mi* (after vowel/consonant) needs to be attached to the most relevant word. When repeating the question in a negative answer, the suffix *-chu* is attached to the most relevant word, while the assertive suffix is attached to the word *mana*, 'no', becoming *mana-n*.

Are you (sg) married?	*¿Kasaru-**chu** ka-nki?* (lit: married-int are-you_sg)
Yes, I'm married.	*Arí, kasaru-**n** ka-ni.* (lit: yes married-assert be-I)
No, I'm not married.	*Mana-**n** kasaru-**chu** ka-ni.* (lit: no-assert married-neg be-I)

Question Words

What?	*¿Ima?*
What's that?	*¿Ima-taq chay?*
	¿Ima-n chay?
Who?	*¿Pi?*
Who's that woman?	*¿Pi-taq chay warmi?*
Whose?	*¿Pi-q?*
Whose car is that?	*¿Pi-q-taq chay awtu?*
Where?	*¿May?*
Where are you going?	*¿May-ta-n ri-sha-nki?*
Where are you from?	*¿May-manta-n ka-nki?*
Which?	*¿Mayqin?*
Which market do you like?	*¿Mayqin qhatu-ta-taq muna-nki?*
How?	*¿Imayna?*
How are you?	*¿Imayna-taq ka-sha-nki?*
How much?/How many?	*¿Hayk'a?*
How much is that bag, Madam?	*¿Hayk'a-taq chay waya-qa, mamitáy?*
When?	*¿Hayk'aq?*
When are we going?	*¿Hayk'aq-mi ripu-ku-sun?*
Why?	*¿Imarayku?/¿Imanaqtin?/ ¿Imanasqa?*
Why is there no car?	*¿Imarayku-n mana karru ka-nchu?*

GRAMMAR

Information Questions

With all standard question words, the final suffix *-n/-mi* or *-taq* should be added. If in doubt about endings, use *-taq*.

NEGATIVES

There are two words to express negation. The first one is *mana* (or *mana-n* when asserting something), 'no/not', in conjunction with the negative suffix *-chu*. The second one is *ama*, 'don't', used in negative commands (see Imperatives page 35). Both of them are placed at the beginning of a sentence, while the placement of the suffix *-chu* varies as it's attached to the most relevant word of the sentence.

I don't speak Quechua.	*(Nuqa) mana-n runasimi-ta rima-ni-chu.* (lit: I no-assert Quechua-obj speak-I-neg)
Don't travel alone.	*Ama sapalla-yki puri-y-chu.* (lit: don't alone-you_sg travel-imp-neg)

PREPOSITIONS

Prepositions are expressed through certain dependent suffixes as well as some individual words. For more information, see Suffixes, page 18.

after	*chaymanta/hinaspa/qhipata*
among	*-pura*
because (of)	*-rayku*
during	*-pi*
for	*-paq*
from	*-manta*
in (location)	*-pi*
to/towards	*-man*
until (time/place)	*-kama*
with	*-wan*
without ...	*mana ...-yuq* (used with a noun only)

GRAMMAR

CONJUNCTIONS

Conjunctions are words or phrases that join concepts or parts of sentences.

In Quechua, most conjunctions are individual words rather than suffixes, but there's one exception: *-pis* or *-pas* (used interchangeably) meaning 'also/and/too'. This suffix is added to verbs or nouns as the very last suffix.

You can go to Arequipa by car and by train.	*Karru-wan-**pis** trin-wan-**pis** runa-kuna Arikipa-ta ri-nku.* (lit: car-with-and train-with-and person-pl Arequipa-to go-they)
Me too.	*Nuqa-**pis**.* (lit: I-too)

after(wards)	*chay-qa/chay-man/chay-pa/ qhipa-n-ta*
and/too/also	*-pis/-pas*
because	*-rayku*
but	*icha-qa*
even so/then	*chay-pacha-pas*
finally	*tuku-na-paq-taq/p'uchuka-y-pi*
first (of all)	*ñawpa-q(-ta)*
however	*chay-puwan-pas*
instead	*aswan(-pas)*
nevertheless	*chay-puwan-pas*
next	*chay-qa/chay-man/chay-pa/ qhipa-n-ta*
or	*icha/utaq*
rather	*aswan(-pas)/icha-qa*
so/therefore	*chay-rayku/nis-paqa/chay-mi*

RIQSINAKUY
MEETING PEOPLE

When initiating conversations in Quechua, you should be aware that since the time of the Conquest, Spanish speakers have often considered themselves superior to Quechua speakers. One form of discrimination has been a refusal by Spanish speakers to use Quechua at all. If you're in a monolingual Quechua community, there'll be no problem with jumping right in, but if in doubt, try asking in Spanish first:

Do you speak Quechua?
¿Habla usted Quechua?   hah·blah *oo*·sted ke·chwa?

YOU SHOULD KNOW   ### YACHANAYKIN
Yes.	ah·*ree*	*Arí.*
No.	*mah*·nah	*Mana.*
Please.	ah·*lyee*·choo	*Allichu.*
Thank you.	sool·*pai*·kee	*Sulpayki.*

GREETINGS & GOODBYES   ### NAPAYKUYKUNAPAS KACHARPARIKUNAPAS

Greetings and farewells are essential elements of social interaction, and you'll be considered rude if you don't use them. Both greetings and goodbyes should be accompanied by a handshake or a hug. When saying goodbye, a simple wave of the hand is appropriate when you're already at a distance.

Good morning.	*wee*·noos *dee*·ahs	*Wuynus diyas.*
Good day. (noon)	*ah*·lyeen *p'oon*·chai;	*Allin p'unchay.*
	ah·lyeen *p'oon*·chow.	*Allin p'unchaw.*
Good afternoon.	*wee*·nahs *tahr*·dis	*Wuynas tardis.*
Good evening/	*wee*·nahs *noo*·chis;	*Wuynas nuchis;*
night.	*ah*·lyeen *too*·tah	*Allin tuta.*
Hello/Hi.	ree·mai·koo·*lyai*·kee/	*Rimaykullayki/*
	nah·pai·koo·*lyai*·kee	*Napaykullayki.*
Goodbye.	hokh koo·tee·*kah*·mah;	*Huq kutikama;*
	too·pah·nahn·chees·*kah*·mah	*Tupananchis-kama.*
Bye.	rah·too·*kah*·mah	*Ratukama.*

CIVILITIES YUPAYCHAKUYKUNA

The Quechua people are generally friendly, helpful, respectful people. Reciprocity is a very important feature of good manners in the Andes. If you ask something of someone, you should be willing to offer in return a small gift, like a souvenir from your home country, or a tip.

Please.	ah·*lyee*·choo	*Allichu.*
Thank you	ah·nyai·*chai*·kee/	*Añaychayki/*
(very much).	sool·*pai*·kee	*Sulpayki*
	(ahn·*chah*·tah)	*(anchata)*
	ah·grah·dee·*see*·kee	*agradisiyki.*
You're welcome.	ee·mah·*mahn*·tah;	*Imamanta;*
	mah·nah	*Mana*
	ee·mah·mahn·*tah*·pahs	*imamantapas.*
Excuse me.	dees·peen·sah·*yoo*·wai	*Dispinsayuway.*
Sorry.	pahm·pah·chah·*yoo*·wai	*Pampachayuway.*

FORMS OF ADDRESS

IMAHINA RUNAKUNA NINAKUSQAN

In Quechua, different forms of address represent different degrees of familiarity, or the age of the person being addressed.

As a foreigner in Quechua-speaking territory, the safest form of address for you to use with a Quechua speaker is *Tayta*, tai·tah, or *taytáy*, tai·*tai*, 'Sir/Mister' for men, and *Mama*, mah·mah, or *mamáy*, mah·*mai*, 'Madam/Mrs' for women, followed by their first name if you know it: *Tayta Satuku* or *Mama Marsilina*.

| Madam/Mrs | mah·mah/mah·mai/ mah·mah·lyai/ mah·mee·tai/ doo·nyah/see·nyoo·rah | Mama/mamáy/ mamallály/ mamitáy/ Duña/Siñura |
| Sir/Mr | tai·tah/tai·tai/ tai·tah·lyai/pah·pai/ wee·rah·ko·chah/ doon/see·nyoor | Tayta/taytáy/ taytallály/papáy/ Wiraqucha/ Dun/Siñur |

Note that if you're writing to someone, the forms *Duña, Siñura, Mama* for women and *Dun, Siñur, Tayta* and *Wiraqucha* for men, all have a capital. While *Mama* and *Tayta* must be used with a proper name, *Wiraqucha* can also be used without one. The forms *mamáy, mamallály, mamitáy, taytáy, taytallály* and *papáy* are not used with proper names.

FOR THE PEOPLE

Many Quechua speakers call themselves *runa*, roo·nah, which means 'the people'. The Spanish terms *indio/india* (m/f) or *cholo/chola* (m/f) are used by some Latin Americans to refer to the indigenous people. These names are derogatory, so don't use them. Instead, use the Spanish *indígena*, 'indigenous person' or *campesino/campesina* (m/f), meaning 'a farmer/farm labourer; a person living in a rural area'.

Miss		
to a young woman	*see*·pahs/*p'ahs*·nyah	*sipas/p'asña*
to a girl	see·*pahs*·chah/	*sipascha/*
	p'ahs·*nyah*·chah	*p'asñacha*
young man		
to an adolescent	*mahkh*·t'ah	*maqt'a*
to a young boy	mahkh·*t'ah*·chah	*maqt'acha*
little girl/boy	wahr·*mah*·chah	*warmacha*

APOLOGIES   PAMPACHAYKUNA

Excuse me. (apology)
   pahm·pah·chah·*yoo*·wai/
   dees·peen·sah·*yoo*·wai
                           Pampachayuway/
                           Dispinsayuway.

Excuse me. (to get past)
   pah·sai·*koo*·sahkh
                           Pasaykusaq.

It's OK. Never mind.
   ah·*lyeen*·mee.
   ***ah·ïnah lyah·kee·kui·*choo**
                           Allinmi.
                           Ama llakikuychu.

HEY YOU!

¡Yaw!, **yow!**, is an informal way to attract someone's attention, similar to 'Hey!' in English. It's usually combined with someone's name or one of the forms of address we've mentioned. It would be considered rude to use it with an adult, or someone you don't know.

People may call you *ringu/gringu* (m), **reen·goo/ green·goo**, 'gringo', or *ringa/gringa* (f), **reen·gah/ green·gah**, 'gringa', if they don't know your name. In recent decades in Latin America, these terms have lost their derogatory connotations, and are now terms of respect. If someone knows your name, they might preface it with *Dun/Siñur/Tayta/Wiraqucha* (m) or *Duña/Siñura* (f) – all terms that refer to pale-skinned foreigners.

BODY LANGUAGE
ÑAWIWAN, MAKIWAN, UMAWAN RIMAY

Quechua speakers are generally humble and may not look you in the eye when speaking. This is more common in rural areas, where visitors are still rare. In metropolitan areas, where people are familiar with foreign tourists, they're more open and less self-effacing. In tourist areas, as you'd expect, vendors have no hesitation in approaching you with their wares or taking you by the arm to try to convince you to buy something.

¡UPSIDE DOWN, RIGHT SIDE UP!

Many punctuation and spelling conventions used in Spanish have been adopted for use in written Quechua too. Questions *start* with an inverted question mark and end in a normal one; the same goes for exclamations ...!

FIRST ENCOUNTERS
ÑAWPAQ TUPANAKUY

You may find that people may not initiate conversations, or might wait to speak until they're sure that you've finished speaking – but don't hesitate to strike up a conversation, as people are very willing to talk to you once you've shown some interest.

How are you?
  ee·mai·*nah*·lyahn kah·*shahn*·kee?   ¿Imaynallan kashanki?
Fine. And you?
  ah·lyee·*lyahn*·mee. kahn·*ree*?   Allillanmi. ¿Qanrí?
What's your name?
  ee·mahn soo·*tee*·kee?   ¿Iman sutiyki?
My name is ...
  ...·n *soo*·tee   ...-n sutiy.
I'd like to introduce you to ...
  ...·wahn rekh·see·nah·*kui*·chees   ...-wan riqsinakuychis.
I'm pleased to meet you.
  ahn·*chah*·tahn koo·see·*koo*·nee   Anchatan kusikuni
  rekh·sees·*pai*·kee   riqsispayki.

MAKING CONVERSATION

IMALLAMANTAPAS RIMAY

Talking about the weather, local food and customs, or asking directions, are always safe openers. Personal questions about age, marital status, income and plans for the day are also perfectly acceptable in Quechua societies. If you're uncomfortable discussing such topics, steer the conversation in another direction, perhaps by answering with a little joke – 'I'm very old', *Sinchi machuñan kani*, *seen·chee mah·choo·*nyahn *kah·*nee, or 'I make enough money to travel once in a while', *Mayninpi purinallaypaqmi qulqita tarini*, mai·*neen·*pee poo·ree·nah·lyai·*pahkh·*mee kol·*ke·*tah tah·*ree·*nee.

Great day, isn't it?
  *soo·*mahkh p'oon·chai,
  *ree·*kee?

*Sumaq p'unchay,
¿riki?*

It's cold/hot today, isn't it?
  ahn·*chah·*tah chee·*ree·*shahn/
  roo·*p·hah·*shahn ree·kee?

*Anchata chirishan/
ruphashan, ¿riki?*

Are you waiting too?
  *kahm·*pees
  soo·yah·ree·shahn·*kee·*choo?

*¿Qampis
suyarishankichu?*

Where are you going?
  mai·*tah·*tahkh ree·*shahn·*kee?

¿Maytataq rishanki?

What are you doing?
  ee·mah·*tah·*tahkh
  ru·wah·*shahn·*kee?

*¿Imatataq
ruwashanki?*

What's this called?
  ee·*mah·*tahkh kai·*pah
  *soo·*teen?

*¿Imataq kaypa
sutin?*

SAY CHEESE & THANK YOU

If you want to take pictures of indigenous people, ask their permission first. It would be considered rude not to offer some little thank-you gift afterwards. In fact, don't be surprised if you're asked outright for some cash!

Can I take a photo (of you)?
ah·*lyee*·choo p-hoo·*too*·tah
hor·koy·kee·*mahn*·choo?
¿*Allichu phututa
hurquykimanchu?*

Beautiful!
soo·mahkh!/ah·nyah·*nyow!*
¡Sumaq!/¡Añañáw!

What a beautiful village this is!
ee·ma *soo*·makh *lyakh*·ta!
¡Ima sumaq llaqta!

It's great here.
ahn·chah ah·*lyeen*·mee
kai·pee
*Ancha allinmi
kaypi.*

I'm here ...   ...·n *kai*·pee   ...-n kaypi
                    kah·*shah*·nee   kashani.
  for a holiday   *how*·kai   hawkay
  (vacation)   pah·chah·*rai*·koo   pacharayku
  on business   lyahn·k'ah·nai·*rai*·koo   llank'anayrayku
  to study   yah·chah·nai·*rai*·koo   yachanayrayku

How long are you here for?
    hai·k'ahkh·*kah*·mahn
    kai·pee kahn·kee?
                         ¿Hayk'aqkaman
                         kaypi kanki?

I'm here for ... weeks/days.
    no·kah ... see·*mah*·nah/
    p'oon·chai *kai*·pee *kah*·sahkh
                         Nuqa ... simana/
                         p'unchay kaypi kasaq.

We're here for ... weeks/days.
    no·*kai*·koo ... see·*mah*·nah/
    p'oon·chai *kai*·pee
    kah·*sahkh*·koo
                         Nuqayku ... simana/
                         p'unchay kaypi
                         kasaqku.

NATIONALITIES   **TUKUY RIKCH'AQ LLAQTAYUQKUNA**

You'll find that many country names in Quechua are similar to English.

Where are you from?
    mai·*mahn*·tahn *kahn*·kee?
                         ¿Maymantan kanki?

I'm from ...	*no*·kah ...·*mahn*·tah *kah*·nee	*Nuqa ...-manta kani.*
We're from ...	no·*kai*·koo ...·*mahn*·tah *kai*·koo	*Nuqayku ...-manta kayku.*
Australia	ows·*trah*·lyah	*Awstraliya*
Canada	kah·*nah*·dah	*Kanada*
England	een·lah·*tee*·rah	*Inlatira*
Europe	yoo·*roo*·pah	*Yurupa*
India	*een*·dyah	*Indya*
Ireland	eer·*lahn*·dah	*Irlanda*
Japan	*hah*·pun	*Hapun*
New Zealand	nui·wah	*Nuywa*
	see·*lahn*·dyah	*Silandya*
Scotland	ees·*koo*·syah	*Iskusya*
the USA	ees·*tah*·doos	*Istadus*
	oo·*nee*·dus	*Unidus*
Wales	*gah*·lees	*Galis*

I live in/by the/a ...	*no·kah ...·pee tee·yah·nee*	*Nuqa ...-pi tiyani.*
city	*lyahkh·tah*	*llaqta*
coast	*koos·tah*	*kusta*
countryside	hah·wah·*lyahkh·tah*	*hawallaqta*
mountains	or·ko·*koo·*nah	*urqukuna*
village	*lyahkh·tah*	*llaqta*

CULTURAL DIFFERENCES
SAPAQ YACHASQANCHISKUNA

Andeans are very generous, and if you express appreciation for something in someone's home, like a throw rug, a ceramic piece or some decoration, they might offer it to you as a gift. To avoid causing offence, gratefully accept the offer. The same is true for offers of food and drink.

If you're in a community during a celebration, people will make every effort to get you to participate, especially in activities such as dancing. It's not considered rude to resist such efforts, but be prepared for persistent attempts to involve you!

THE ANDEAN WAVE

If you want to beckon an Andean to you, hold your hand palm out, facing the other person, and waggle your fingers without moving the rest of your arm, as if you were waving goodbye to a child. If you wave your arm from side to side this will be understood as a goodbye gesture, as it generally is in Western cultures.

MEETING PEOPLE

How do you do this
in your country?
ee·mai·*nah*·tahkh
lyahkh·tai·*kee*·pee *kai*·tah
roo·wai·*kee*·chees?

¡Imaynataq
llaqtaykipi kayta
ruwaykichis?

Is this a local or national custom?
wah·keen
lyahkh·tah·*koo*·nahkh ee·chah
lyoo lyahkh·tah·*koo*·nahkh
kow·sai·neen·*koo*·choo chai?

¿Wakin
llaqtakunaq icha
lliw llaqtakunaq
kawsayninkuchu chay?

I'm sorry Sir/Madam,
it's not the custom in my country.
pahm·pah·chai·*koo*·wai
tai·*tail*/mah·*mai*, mah·*nahn*
lyahkh·*tai*·pah *chai*·tah
kow·sai·*neen*·choo

Pampachaykuway
taytáy/mamáy, manan
llaqtaypa chayta
kawsayninchu.

Please don't be offended.
ah·*lyee*·choo ah·mah
p-hee·nyah·*kui*·choo

Allichu ama
phiñakuychu.

I don't mind watching, but
I'd prefer not to participate.
k-hah·*wai*·tah
k-hah·wai·*mahn*·mee,
ee·*chah*·kah mah·nahn
chai·tah roo·*wai*·tah
moo·nai·*mahn*·choo

Qhawayta
qhawaymanmi,
ichaqa manan
chayta ruwayta
munaymanchu.

(But) I'll give it a go.
(ee·*chah*·kah)
ah·tee·pahs·kah·*lyai*·tah
roo·wai·*koo*·sahkh

(Ichaqa)
atipasqallayta
ruwaykusaq.

Let's dance!
too·*soo*·soon!

¡Tususun!

I don't know how to dance.
mah·nahn too·*sui*·tah
yah·chah·*nee*·choo

Manan tusuyta
yachanichu.

THANKS!

There are two ways to say thank you in Quechua, the traditional 'Sulpáy', sool·pai, and 'Añay', ah·nyai, which is increasingly popular these days.

local	kai lyahkh·*tah*·pee	*kay llaqta*
national	lyoo	*lliw*
	lyahkh·tah·koo·*nah*·pee	*llaqtakunapi*
everybody	*lyah*·pahn/lyah·*pahn*·koo	*llapan/llapanku*

AGE   WATA

How old are you, Sir/Ma'am? (to adult)	*hai*·k'ah wah·tah·*yokh*·mee *kahm*·kee, tai·*tail*mah·*mai?*	*¿Hayk'a watayuqmi kanki, taytáy/mamáy?*
How old is your child? (to mother)	*hai*·k'ah wah·tah·*yokh*·mee wah·*wai*·kee?	*¿Hayk'a watayuqmi wawayki?*
How old are you? (to child)	*hai*·k'ah wah·tah·chah·*yokh*·mee *kahm*·kee?	*¿Hayk'a watachayuqmi kanki?*
I'm ... years old.	*no*·kah ... wah·tah·*yokh*·mee *kah*·nee	*Nuqa ... watayuqmi kani.*

(See Numbers & Amounts for your age, page 167.)

MEETING PEOPLE

OCCUPATIONS

What do you do?
ee·*mah*·peen lyahn·*k'ahn*·kee
kai·pee?

I'm a/an ...
no·kah ...·n/·mee *kah*·nee

RUWANAKUNA

¿Imapin llank'anki
kaypi?

Nuqa ...-n/-mi kani.

aide/assistant	yah·*nah*·pahkh/ yah·nah·*pah*·kokh	yanapaq/ yanapakuq
artist	ahr·*tees*·tah	artista
businessperson	*rahn*·tekh/*k-hah*·tokh/ teen·*dah*·yokh	rantiq/qhatuq/ tindayuq
carpenter	kahr·peen·*tee*·roo	karpintiru
chef	wai·k'okh/ wai·k'oo·*pah*·kokh	wayk'uq/ wayk'upakuq
community leader	kah·*mah*·chekh	kamachiq
craftsperson	ahr·tee·*sah*·noo	artisanu
dancer	*too*·sokh	tusuq
doctor	*dook*·toor	duktur
driver	*choo*·feer	chufir
engineer	een·hee·*nyee*·roo	inhiniru
farmer	*chahkh*·rah *roo*·nah	chakra runa
fisherman	*chahly*·wah *hah*·p'ekh	challwa hap'iq
fortune teller	*wah*·tokh	watuq
healer	*hahm*·pekh	hampiq
journalist	peer·yoo·*dees*·tah	piryudista
labourer	*lyahn*·k'akh	llank'aq
lawyer	*yoo*·yai kokh/ ah·woo·*gah*·roo	yuyay quq/ awugaru
mayor	ahl·*kahl*·dee	alkaldi
mechanic	mee·kah·*nee*·koo	mikaniku
minister (pastor)	*roo*·nah *mee*·chekh	runa michiq
nurse	*on*·kokh yah·*nah*·pahkh	unquq yanapaq
office worker	oo·fee·see·*nah*·pee *lyahn*·k'akh	ufisinapi llank'aq

police officer	wahr·*dee*·yah	*wardiya*
priest	*tai*·tah koo·rah	*tayta kura*
scientist	hah·*mow*·t'ah	*hamawt'a*
shepherd	*mee*·chekh	*michiq*
singer	*tah*·kekh	*takiq*
student	*yah*·chai *moo*·nahkh	*yachay munaq*
teacher	yah·*chah*·chekh	*yachachiq*
university lecturer/ professor	hah·*mow*·t'ah	*hamawt'a*
waiter	mee·*k-hoo*·nah	*mikhuna*
	wah·*see*·pee	*wasipi*
	lyahn·k'ahkh	*llank'aq*
writer	*kel*·kahkh	*qilqaq*

I'm retired.
mah·*nah*·nyahn
lyahn·k'ah·*nee*·choo,
sah·mah·koo·*nee*·nyahn
Manañan llank'anichu, samakuniñan.

I'm unemployed.
mah·nah lyahn·k'ai·*nee*·yokh *kah*·nee
Mana llank'ayniyuq kani.

What are you studying?
ee·*mah*·tahkh
yah·chah·*shahn*·kee?
¿Imatataq yachashanki?

I'm studying ...	*no*·kah ...·tahn yah·chah·*shah*·nee	*Nuqa ...-tan yachashani.*
art	*ahr*·tee	*arti*
arts/humanities	ee·mai·*mah*·nah yoo·yai·*koo*·nah	*imaymana yuyaykuna*
engineering	een·hee·nyee·*ree*·yah	*inhiñiriya*
English	*een*·lees	*inlis*
languages	ee·mai·*mah*·nah see·mee·*koo*·nah	*imaymana simikuna*
medicine	mee·dee·*see*·nah	*midisina*
science	hah·*moo*·t'ai	*hamut'ay*
Spanish	kahs·tee·*lyah*·noo	*kastillanu*

FEELINGS   SINTIMINTUKUNA

If someone asks, 'How are you?', your first response should be a
generic 'I'm well' or 'I'm not well'.

How are you?
  ee·mai·*nah*·lyahn kah·*shahn*·kee?   *¿Imaynallan kashanki?*
I'm well.
  ah·*lyeen*·lyahn kah·*shah*·nee   *Allinllan kashani.*
I'm not so good.
  mah·nahn ah·*lyeen*·choo   *Manan allinchu*
  kah·*shah*·nee   *kashani.*

Are you ...?   ...choo kah·*shahn*·kee?   *¿...-chu kashanki?*
I'm ...   ...n kah·*shah*·nee   *...-n kashani.*
  afraid   mahn·*chahs*·kah   *manchasqa*
  angry   fee·*nyahs*·kah   *piñasqa*
  depressed   pee·see·*chahs*·kah   *pisichasqa*
  grateful   son·kon·chah·*koos*·kah   *sunqunchakusqa*
  happy   koo·*sees*·kah   *kusisqa*
  in a hurry   ah·poo·*rahs*·kah   *apurasqa*
  inspired   kahly·pah·chah·*koos*·kah   *kallpachakusqa*
  sad   lyah·*kees*·kah   *llakisqa*
  tired   sai·*k'oos*·kah   *sayk'usqa*
  worried   lyah·*kees*·kah   *llakisqa*

A phrase such as 'I'm afraid' is easy enough to translate from
English to Quechua, but 'I'm cold' is more problematic. These
feelings require special phrases to express them:

I'm cold.
  chee·ree·wah·*shahn*·mee   *Chiriwashanmi.*
I'm hot.
  roo·p·hah·ree·wah·   *Ruphariwa-*
  shahn·mee   *shanmi.*
I'm hungry.
  yahr·kah·wah·*shahn*·mee   *Yarqawashanmi.*

I'm thirsty.
ch'ah·kee·wah·*shahn*·mee   *Ch'akiwashanmi.*
I'm sleepy.
poo·*nyui*·mee   *Puñuymi*
ai·sah·*wah*·shahn   *aysawashan.*
I'm right. (correct)
rah·soon·nee·*yokh*·mee   *Rasunniyuqmi*
kah·nee   *kani.*
I'm sorry. (condolence)
ahn·*chah*·tahn   *Anchatan*
lyah·kee·*pai*·kee   *llakipayki.*

BREAKING THE LANGUAGE BARRIER

RIMANAKUYTA ATIY

Do you speak ...?   ... ree·mahn·*kee*·choo?   *¿... rimankichu?*
    English   een·*lees*·tah   *inlista*
    Quechua   roo·nah·see·*mee*·tah   *runasimita*
    Spanish   kahs·tee·lyah·*noo*·tah   *kastillanuta*

Yes, I do.
ah·*ree*, ree·*mah*·neen   *Arí, rimanin.*
No, I don't.
mah·nahn, ree·mah·*nee*·choo   *Manan, rimanichu.*
I speak a little bit.
no·kah pee·see·*lyah*·tah   *Nuqa pisillata*
ree·*mah*·nee   *rimani.*
Who speaks English here?
pee·tahkh *kai*·pee   *¿Pitaq kaypi*
een·*lees*·tah *ree*·mahn?   *inlista riman?*

MEETING PEOPLE

Do you understand?
  een·teen·deen·*kee*·choo?   *¿Intindinkichu?*
I (don't) understand.
  (*mah*·nahn)   (*Manan*)
  een·teen·dee·*nee*·choo   *intindinichu.*
Could you speak more slowly?
  ah·lyee·lyah·*mahn*·tah   *¿Allillamanta*
  ree·mai·koon·kee·*mahn*·choo?   *rimaykunkimanchu?*
Could you repeat that?
  yah·pah·*mahn*·tah *chai*·tah   *¿Yapamanta chayta*
  ree·mai·koon·kee·*mahn*·choo?   *rimaykunkimanchu?*
Please write it down.
  ah·*lyee*·choo *kel*·kai   *Allichu qilqay.*
How do you say this in Quechua?
(when pointing to something)
  ee·mah·neen·*chees*·mee   *¿Imaninchismi*
  kai·tah roo·nah·see·*mee*·pee?   *kayta runasimipi?*
What does ... mean?
  ee·mah nee·nahn·*chees*·mee ...?   *¿Ima ninanchismi ...?*

RELIGION   RILIHIYUN

Religion is a topic of everyday conversation – it's certainly not a taboo subject. While the Andean countries are officially Catholic, there's actually a fair amount of freedom of religion. All of the Christian religions are represented, as well as many Eastern religions and beliefs. Names of religions were simply borrowed from Spanish and adapted to the Quechua pronunciation system.

What's your religion?
  ee·*mah*·tahkh   *¿Imataq*
  ree·lee·hee·yun·*nee*·kee?   *rilihiyunniyki?*

I'm (a/an) ...   *no·*kah *...n/·*mee   *Nuqa ...-n/·mi*
                *kah·*nee   *kani.*

Adventist	ahd·ween·*tees*·tah	*adwintista*
Baptist	wow·*tees*·tah	*wawtista*
Buddhist	woo·*dees*·tah	*wudista*
Christian	krees·tee·*yah*·noo	*kristiyanu*
Evangelist	ee·wahn·hee·*lees*·tah	*iwanhilista*
Hindu	*een*·doo	*indu*
Jehovah's Witness	ee·wahn·hee·*lees*·tah	*iwanhilista*
Jewish	hoo·*dee*·yoo	*hudiyu*
Lutheran	loo·tee·*rah*·noo	*lutiranu*
Methodist	mee·too·*dees*·tah	*mitudista*
Mormon	*moor*·moon	*murmun*
Muslim	moo·*sool*·mahn	*musulman*
Protestant	proo·tees·*tahn*·tee	*prutistanti*

I'm not religious.
  *mah·*nah   *Mana*
  ree·lee·hee·yoon·nee·*yokh·*mee *rilihiyunniyuqmi*
  *kah·*nee   *kani.*

IT'S THE END OF THE WORD

When using *-n/-mi*, choose the *-n* ending when the preceding root word ends in a vowel, and the *-mi* ending when it ends in a consonant: eg, *adwintista-n*, ahd·ween·*tees*·tahn, or *murmun-mi*, moor·*moon*·mee. Note that using the *-mi* ending will change which syllable is stressed.

COSMOVISION & CATHOLICISM

Catholicism as practised by the indigenous people in the Andes has some intriguing differences from Western Catholicism.

The Andean religion, before the conquistadors introduced Christianity, was more a cosmovision than simply a religion – it was an entire way of viewing the world and explaining natural events. It was animistic, believing that animals and other elements of the natural world have souls. The highest deity was 'Father Sun', *Tayta Inti*, *tai·tah een·tee*, from whom the Incas believed themselves to be directly descended.

Obviously the Incas had great respect for the natural world and its power. Their sacred objects, or *wak'as*, *wah·k'ahs*, were mountain peaks, rivers and lakes, all of whose souls needed to be appeased regularly with ritual offerings, usually of food or drink. *Pachamama*, *pah·chah·mah·mah*, was 'Mother Earth', the nurturing protector and life-giver of all beings, and it was particularly important to pay her for her bounty. This was done through a major celebration that took place every August, known as 'payment to Mother Earth' or *haywakuy*, *hai·wah·kui*. Payments consisted of offerings of coca leaves, food or beverages.

When the Spaniards arrived (1532), they began to convert the locals to Catholicism. The Andeans seemed to accept the teaching of the missionaries fairly readily but, in reality, they did not reject their previous beliefs to accept the new ones. Rather, they syncretised them, or layered

COSMOVISION & CATHOLICISM

them on top of their existing beliefs. The Christian belief in heaven and hell led them to add similar spiritual territories to their organisational schema of the world. In addition to *kay pacha*, kai *pah·chah*, the world in which people dwell, there is *hanaq pacha*, *hah·nahkh pah·chah*, the world above, where the gods dwell, and *ukhu pacha*, *oo·k-hoo pah·chah*, the world below, a world of shadows and darkness. In the Andean cosmology, these three worlds interconnect and their inhabitants interact.

Another example of this syncretism is the Andean belief in God and active worship of the saints. They consider Jesus and the Virgin Mary to belong to this category of saints. Interestingly, they have blended the identities of the Catholic saints with their own *apus*, *ah·poos*, 'principal mountain gods' and *wak'as*, *wah·k'ahs*, 'sacred places'. This was a logical thing to do. For Western Catholics, the saints serve as intermediaries between humans and their God, and in the ancient Andean cosmovision, the *apus* and *wak'as* also served an intermediary function. The Virgin Mary herself came to be associated with *Pachamama*, the Earth Mother, the greatest of all female deities.

The most obvious manifestation of this practice is the habit of putting crosses on mountain tops, and holding traditional festivals on Catholic saints' days, so that the 'Spanish' God and saints and the traditional mountain *apus* and *wak'as* can be worshipped at the same time.

I'm Catholic, but I don't
go to mass.
    kah·too·*lee*·koon *kah*·nee,
    mah·*nah*·tahkh
    mee·*sah*·mahn ree·*nee*·choo

Katulikun kani,
manataq
misaman rinichu.

I believe in God.
    tai·tah dee·yoos·*mahn*·mee
    ee·*nyee*·nee

Tayta Diyusmanmi
iñini.

I'm interested in astrology.
    koy·lyoor·koo·nah·*mahn*·tah
    yah·*chai*·tah moo·*nah*·nee

Quyllurkunamanta
yachayta munani.

I'm interested in philosophy.
    hah·moo·t'ai·*mahn*·tah
    yah·*chai*·tah moo·*nah*·nee

Hamut'aymanta
yachayta munani.

I'm an atheist.
    mah·nahn dee·*yoos*·mahn
    ee·nyee·*nee*·choo

Manan Diyusman
iñinichu.

Can I attend this service/mass?
    kai kool·*too*·tah/mee·*sah*·tah
    oo·yah·ree·*mahn*·choo?

¿Kay kultuta/misata
uyarimanchu?

Can I pray here?
    mah·nyah·kui·*mahn*·choo
    kai·pee?

¿Mañakuymanchu
kaypi?

Where can I pray/worship?
    mai·*pee*·tahkh
    yoo·pai·*chai*·mahn?

¿Maypitaq
yupaychayman?

Is there a church here?
    kahn·choo een·*lee*·sah *kai*·pee?

¿Kanchu inlisa kaypi?

ancestor	*nyow*·pah *ai*·lyoo	*ñawpa ayllu*
baptism	oo·*lee*·yai	*uliyay*
christening	wow·*tee*·sai	*wawtisay*
church	een·*lee*·sah;	*inlisa;*
	dee·*yoos*·pah *wah*·seen	*Diyuspa wasin*
cross	*koo*·roos	*kurus*
deity	*dee*·yoos *kai*·neen	*Diyus kaynin*
devil	*sahkh*·rah/*soo*·pai	*saqra/supay*
evil spirit	*so*·k'ah	*suq'a*
Father Sun	*tai*·tah een·tee	*Tayta Inti*
Festival of the Sun	een·tee *rai*·mee	*Inti Raymi*
God	*dee*·yoos/*yah*·yah	*Diyus/Yaya*
creator of the Earth	pah·chah·*kah*·mahkh	*Pachakamaq*
creator of the Incas	wee·rah·*ko*·chah	*Wiraqucha*
mountain god	*ah*·poo	*Apu*
secondary mountain gods	*ow*·kee	*awki*
Incan priest	*oo*·moo	*umu*
lake	*mah*·mah ko·chah	*Mama Qucha*
lightning	ee·*lyah*·pah	*illapa*
mass	*mee*·sah	*misa*
Mother Earth	pah·chah·*mah*·mah	*Pachamama*
Mother Moon	*mah*·mah kee·lyah	*Mama Killa*
to pray	mah·*nyah*·kui	*mañakuy*
prayer	mah·*nyah*·kokh	*mañakuq*
priest	*tai*·tah koo·rah; *yah*·yah	*tayta kura; yaya*
procession	proo·*see*·yoon	*prusiyun*
river	*mah*·yoo	*mayu*
sabbath	yoo·pai·*chah*·nah	*yupaychana*
	poon·ch'ai	*punch'ay*
sacred place	*wah*·k'ah	*wak'a*
sacrifice	*hai*·wai	*hayway*

saint (m/f)	tai·*tah*·chah/	*taytacha*/
	mah·*mah*·chah	*mamacha*
shrine	kah·*pee*·lyah	*kapilla*
sin	*hoo*·chah	*hucha*
to sin	hoo·chah·*lyee*·kui	*huchallikuy*
stars	koy·lyoor·*koo*·nah	*quyllurkuna*
temple	*mahn*·ko *wah*·see	*manqu wasi*
Temple of the Sun	ko·ree·*kahn*·chah	*Qurikancha*
thunder	*k-hahkh*·yah	*qhaqya*
witch	*lai*·kah	*layqa*

MAYTAPAS RIY
GETTING AROUND

Arranging journeys by plane, train, bus or taxi is generally done in Spanish or English in the Andean region. In Quechua-speaking communities, such forms of transport are not common – even street signs are usually in Spanish.

Nevertheless, Quechua will be the key to seeking your own way in remote areas, if you need to ask whether a car or bus is available, or which way you should go.

FINDING YOUR WAY
MAYTAPAS RIYTA YACHAY

Excuse me Sir/Madam ...
pahm·pah·chah·yoo·wai
*tai·*tai/mah·*mai* ...
Pampachayuway
tayta/mamay ...

Where am I?
mai·peen kah·*shah·*nee?
¿Maypin kashani?

I'm looking for ...
...tahn mahs·k·hah·*shah·*nee
...-tan maskhashani.

Where's the ...?	**mai·**pee·tahk ...?	*¿Maypitaq ...?*
bus station	**oo·**nee·woos sah·yahn	*uniwus sayan*
dock/pier	**wahm·**poo sah·yahn	*wampu sayan*
road to ...	**...**tah ree·*nah·*pahkh nyahn	*...-ta rinapaq ñan*
train station	treen sah·yahn	*trin sayan*

LOCAL TRANSPORT

If you're adventurous, try riding in the back of a pickup truck to get from one place to another. This may be the only way to get off the beaten track. You're exposed to the elements, but it's a great way to see the countryside and get to know the locals. You're expected to offer some sort of payment to the driver, as the Andeans do themselves.

GETTING AROUND

What time does the ... leave?	ee·mah oo·*rah*·tahkh ... lyokh·seen?	¿Ima urataq ... lluqsin?
What time does the ... arrive?	ee·mah oo·*rahs*·mee ... chah·*yah*·moon?	¿Ima urasmi ... chayamun?
boat	*wahm*·poo	wampu
bus	oo·*nee*·woos	uniwus
minibus	oo·nee·*woos*·chah/ *meek*·roo	uniwuscha/ mikru
train	treen	trin

How do we get to ...?
  ee·mai·*nah*·tahkh ...·man   ¿Imaynataq ...-man
  chah·*yahn*·chees?   chayanchis?
Is it close by?
  sees·*pah*·choo?   ¿Sispachu?
Can we walk there?
  chah·kee·*lyah*·wahn   ¿Chakillawan
  ree·koo·*mahn*·choo chai·mahn?   riykumanchu chayman?
Can you show me (on the map)?
  (mah·*pah*·pee)   (Mapapi)
  k·hah·wai·kah·chee·   ¿Qhawaykachi-
  wahn·kee·*mahn*·choo?   wankimanchu?

BUT HOW WILL IT END?

Remember, when adding suffixes to words, choose the *first* ending when the root word ends in a vowel, and the *second* ending when it ends in a consonant.

What's the name of this ...?	ee·*mah*·tahkh kai ...·kh/·pah soo·teen?	¿Imataq kay ...-q/-pa sutin?
city/village	*lyahkh*·tah	llaqta
highway	*pees*·tah	pista
path	nyahn	ñan
road	kah·ree·*tee*·rah	karitira
street	*kah*·lyee	kalli

DIRECTIONS

Straight ahead.
    syookh/dee·*ree*·choo
To the left/right.
    lyoo·*k'ee*·mahn/pah·*nyah*·mahn
Turn at the next corner/street.
    hah·mokh k'oo·*choo*·pee/
    kah·*lyee*·pee moo·*yui*·kui

YACHACHIYKUNA

Siwk/Dirichu.

Lluq'iman/Pañaman.

Hamuq k'uchupi/
kallipi muyuykuy.

across (from)	cheem·*pah*·pee	*chimpapi*
behind	k-*he*·pah	*qhipa*
far	*kah*·roo	*karu*
here	*kai*·pee	*kaypi*
in front (of)	nyow·*pahkh*·pee	*ñawpaqpi*
near	*sees*·pah	*sispa*
there	*chai*·pee/chai·*nekh*·pee/	*chaypi/chayniqpi/*
	hah·*kai*·pee	*haqaypi*

north	*wee·chai*	*wichay*
south	*oo·rai*	*uray*
east	*een·tekh lyokh·see·nahn*	*intiq lluqsinan*
west	*een·tekh cheen·kah·nahn*	*intiq chinkanan*

Thank you for showing us the way.

sool·pai nyahn·tah	*Sulpáy ñanta*
rekh·see·chee·moo·wahs	*riqsichimuwa-*
kai·kee·koo·mahn·tah	*sqaykikumanta.*

For more instructions, see Taxi, below.

ADDRESSES   DIRIKSIYUNKUNA

Addresses are generally indicated in Spanish rather than in Quechua. A typical address might look like this:

> Sra. María Condori Guzmán
> Avenida Tullomayo 428
> Cuzco, Peru

Large cities, such as Lima, La Paz and Quito, may have several postal codes, but this is not common. Post office boxes *(apartado* or *casilla* in Spanish) are popular too:

> Sr. José Huamán Mamani
> Apartado Postal 477 (or Casilla Postal 477)
> Cochabamba, Bolivia

TAXI   TAKSI

Taxis are not widely available in the more rural Quechua-speaking areas. To hold a licence, the driver must speak Spanish, so arrangements are generally made in Spanish – or possibly in English in larger cities.

There are two kinds of taxis. A *taxi oficial* is a state-regulated taxi, which is more likely (but not guaranteed) to have a meter; a *taxi particular* is an informal, privately owned taxi – fares are negotiable. You can flag down either sort in large cities.

Make sure you bargain and settle on a price to your destination before getting in. Taxis are generally inexpensive, but some drivers will raise their prices when dealing with a foreigner. See Bargaining, page 127, for more on this.

Sir/Madam, I want to go to ...
    tai·*tail*mah·*mai* ....tah
    ree·tah moo·*nah*·nee

Taytáy/Mamáy ...-ta
riyta munani.

How much is it to go to ...?
    hai·k'ahn *kwees*·tahn ....tah
    ree·*nah*·pahkh?

¿Hayk'an kwistan ...-ta
rinapaq?

How much is the ticket/fare?
    hai·k'ahn *kwees*·tahn pah·*sah*·hee?

¿Hayk'an kwistan pasahi?

Instructions

Please take me to ...
    ah·*lyee*·choo ....tah ah·*pah*·wai

Yachachiykuna

Allichu ...-ta apaway.

Keep going straight!
    syookh!

¡Siwk!

The next street to the left/right.
    hah·mokh kah·*lyee*·pee
    pah·*nyah*·mahn/lyo·*k'e*·mahn
    moo·*yui*·kui

Hamuq kallipi
pañaman/lluq'iman
muyuykuy.

Please slow down.
    ah·*lyee*·choo
    ah·lyee·lyah·*mahn*·tah ree

Allichu
allillamanta riy.

Please wait here.
    ah·*lyee*·choo *kai*·pee *soo*·yai

Allichu kaypi suyay.

Stop here!
    sah·yai *kai*·pee!

¡Sayay kaypi!

Stop at the corner!
    chai k'hoo·*choo*·pee *sah*·yai!

¡Chay k'uchupi sayay!

BUYING TICKETS   WULITUKUNATA RANTIY

Haggling is common when buying tickets for travel. You can even bargain with a travel agent, but purchasing directly from a bus or train station means paying the posted price. Foreigners will often pay more than locals do, especially in tourist areas. See Bargaining, page 127, for more on this.

    Buying tickets at bus stations is usually done in Spanish. Flight arrangements are always made in Spanish or in English.

Where can I buy a ticket?	
mai·*pee*·tahkh	¿*Maypitaq*
woo·lee·*too*·tah	*wulituta*
rahn·tee·*rui*·mahn?	*rantirquyman?*
How much is the ticket/fare?	
hai·k'ahn kwees·tahn	¿*Hayk'an kwistan*
pah·*sah*·hee?	*pasahi?*
How long does it take to get to ...?	
hai·k'ah oo·rah·*pee*·tahkh	¿*Hayk'a urapitaq*
...mahn chah·*yahn*·chees?	*...-man chayanchis?*

BUS & CAR   UNIWUS, KARRU

Bus services come in a wide range of quality and service levels, and once again, transactions are conducted almost exclusively in Spanish. However, you might want to inform yourself on local bus services – or the availability of a car where there are no buses – by asking local Quechua speakers.

What time does the ... bus arrive?	ee·mah oo·rah·tahkh ... oo·nee·*woos*·kah chah·*yah*·moon?	¿*Ima urataq* ... *uniwusqa chayamun?*
What time does the ... car leave?	ee·mah oo·*rah*·tahkh ... kah·*rroo*·kah *lyok*·seen?	¿*Ima urataq* ... *karruqa lluqsin?*
first	*nyow*·pahkh	*ñawpaq*
last	*k-he*·pah	*qhipa*
next	*hah*·mokh	*hamuq*

GOING MY WAY?

In rural areas where there's little or no public transport available, cars often double as buses. Drivers will be on the lookout for anyone going in the same direction. You'll need to agree on a price before accepting the lift – see Taxi and Buying Tickets (pages 68, 70).

Does this bus/car go to ...?
   kai oo·*nee*·woos/*kah*·rroo ...·mahn *reen*·choo?
   ¿Kay uniwus/karru ...-man rinchu?

How many times a day do buses/cars pass by here?
   ***hai*·k'ah *koo*·teen oo·nee·woos·*koo*·nah/ kah·rroo·*koo*·nah *kai*·pee *pah*·sahn *sah*·pah p'oon·chai?**
   ¿Hayk'a kutin uniwuskuna/ karrukuna kaypi pasan sapa p'unchay?

Where does this bus/car go?
   ***mai*·tahn/mai·*mahn*·mee kai oo·*nee*·woos/*kah*·rroo reen?**
   ¿Maytan/maymanmi kay uniwus/karru rin?

Where's the bus/car stop?
   mai·*pee*·tahkh oo·*nee*·woos/ *kah*·rroo *sah*·yahn?
   ¿Maypitaq uniwus/ karru sayan?

Which bus/car goes to ...?
   ***mai*·ken oo·*nee*·woos·tahkh/ kah·*rroo*·tahkh ...·mahn reen?**
   ¿Mayqin uniwustaq/ karrutaq ...-man rin?

Where can I catch the bus/car to ...?
   mai·*pee*·tahkh ...·mahn ree·*nai*·pahkh oo·*nee*·woos·tah/ kah·*rroo*·tah hah·p'ee·*rui*·mahn?
   ¿Maypitaq ...-man rinaypaq uniwusta/ karruta hap'irquyman?

This is my seat.
   tee·yah·*nai*·mee *kai*·kah
   Tiyanaymi kayqa.

Could you let me know
when we get to ...?
    ah·*lyee*·choo ...·mahn
    chah·yahkh·*teen*·chees
    wee·lyai·koo·wahn·
    kee·*mahn*·choo?

Can you tell the driver to stop?
    ah·*lyee*·choo *sah*·yai
    neen·kee·*mahn*·choo
    choo·feer·*tah*·kah?

I'd like to get off here.
    kai·pee oo·rai·*kui*·tahn
    moo·*nah*·nee

¿Allichu ...-man
chayaqtinchis
willaykuwan-
kimanchu?

¿Allichu sayay
ninkimanchu
chuphirtaqa?

Kaypi uraykuytan
munani.

THE FUN BUS

When travelling on local buses and minibuses, be prepared for an extraordinary acoustic treat and flexible ideas on what constitutes safe driving. Between passengers yelling at the conductor, the conductor yelling out the stops as they come up, and the driver yelling out the window at other drivers, things can get loud. There may be music blasting out through numerous speakers. Local performers might climb on to give an impromptu performance complete with expectations of tips, while local vendors tout their wares. Buses are often overcrowded, especially when animals and food products are on board.

TRAIN   TRIN

Trains don't run nearly as frequently as buses, but they're generally
more comfortable for long-distance travel.

What's the name of this station?
ee·*mah*·tahkh kai   *¿Imataq kay*
sah·*yah*·nahkh soo·teen?   *sayanaq sutin?*

What's the name of the next station?
ee·*mah*·tahkh *hah*·mokh   *¿Imataq hamuq*
sah·*yah*·nahkh soo·teen?   *sayanaq sutin?*

Does this train stop at (Arequipa)?
(ah·ree·kee·*pah*·pee)   *¿(Arikipapi)*
sah·*yahn*·choo kai treen·kah?   *sayanchu kay trinqa?*

There's no train today.
mah·nan treen *kahn*·choo   *Manan trin kanchu*
koo·nahn *p'oon*·chai   *kunan p'unchay.*

Can I sit here?
tee·yai·*mahn*·choo kai·pee?   *¿Tiyaymanchu kaypi?*

I want to get off at ...
...·pee oo·rai·*kui*·tah   *...-pi uraykuyta*
moo·*nah*·nee   *munani.*

BOAT   WAMPU

Boat travel in the Andes might be by canoe for travelling along
rivers and other waterways, or by motor boat or hovercraft when
travelling from island to island on large lakes such as Titicaca.
Even luxury cruise ships, *hatun wampu*, *hah*·toon *wahm*·poo,
are an option, for those wanting to visit the Galapagos Islands.

Arrangements for this type of transport are usually made
through travel agencies, although you may also be able to
negotiate on the spot.

Where can I find a boat that
goes to ...?
mai·*pee*·tahkh wahm·*poo*·tah   *¿Maypitaq wamputa*
tah·ree·*rui*·mahn ....tah   *tarirquyman ...-ta*
ree·*nai*·pahkh?   *rinaypaq?*

Where does that boat go?
**mai·*tah*·tahkh/mai·*mahn*·tahkh
chai *wahm*·poo reen?**

¿Maytataq/Maymantaq
chay wampu rin?

Where does the boat leave from?
**mai·mahn·*tah*·tahkh
wahm·poo lyokh·seen?**

¿Maymantaq
wampu lluqsin?

What time does the boat arrive/leave?
**ee·mah oo·*rahs*·mee *wahm*·poo
chah·*yah*·moon/lyokh·seen?**

¿Ima urasmi wampu
chayamun/lluqsin?

DRIVING   KARRU

Car rentals are generally only available in major cities. If you decide to rent a car, services – from filling up to repairs – will be handled in Spanish.

In the larger cities and tourist areas, motorcycling is also possible. Organised tours are the easiest, but renting or buying your own motorcycle is an option.

Is there a mechanic around here?
**kahn·choo mee·kah·*nee*·koo
kai·pee?**

¿Kanchu mikaniku
kaypi?

Is there a gas/petrol station nearby?
***gree*·foo *kahn*·choo kai·pee?**

¿Griphu kanchu kaypi?

Where can I buy gas/petrol?
**mai·peen gah·soo·lee·*nah*·tah
rahn·tee·*rui*·mahn?**

¿Maypin gasulinata
rantirquyman?

Does this road/highway/path
lead to ...?
**kai kah·ree·*tee*·rah/*pees*·tah/nyahn
...·*mahn*·choo reen?**

¿Kay karitira/pista/ñan
...-manchu rin?

How can I go to ...?
**ee·*mai*·nahn ...·mahn
ree·mahn?**

¿Imaynan ...-man
riyman?

Which is the way to ...?
mai·*neen*·tahn ...·mahn reen?

¿Maynintan ...-man rin?

I'm lost.
***cheen*·kai cheen·*kai*·lyah
poo·ree·*koo*·nee**

Chinkay chinkaylla
purikuni.

My car has broken down.
  kah·*rrui*·kah *mah*·nahn
  poo·*ree*·tah ah·*teen*·choo

*Karruyqa manan
puriyta atinchu.*

Is there a car here going to ...?
  kah·rroo *kahn*·choo kai·pee
  ...mahn ree·*nah*·pahkh?

*¿Karru kanchu kaypi
...-man rinapaq?*

Where are you going?
  mai·tahn ree·*shahn*·kee

¿Maytan rishanki?

I'm going to ...
  ...tahn ree·*shah*·nee

...-tan rishani.

Can you take me there in your car?
  pahkh·tah kah·rrui·*kee*·pee
  ah·pah·wahn·*kee*·mahn
  chai·mahn?

*¿Paqta karruykipi
apawankiman
chayman?*

How much do I owe you?
  hai·k'ah·*tah*·tahkh
  mah·noo·*kui*·kee?

*¿Hayk'atataq
manukuyki?*

BICYCLE   WISIKILITA

Mountain biking is, for obvious reasons, one of the most popular forms of cycling in the Andes. Bicycles are available to rent or buy in larger cities and tourist areas.

Is ... within cycling distance?
  wee·see·kee·lee·*tah*·wahn
  ree·rui·*mahn*·choo ...·mahn?

*¿Wisikilitawan
rirquymanchu ...-man?*

Is there a bike path?
  kahn·choo wee·see·kee·*lee*·tah
  nyahn?

*¿Kanchu wisikilita
ñan?*

Who can show me the bicycle paths?
  pee·tahkh wee·see·kee·*lee*·tah   ¿Pitaq wisikilita
  nyahn·koo·*nah*·tah   ñankunata
  rekh·see·chee·*wahn*·mahn?   riqsichiwanman?
Where can I hire a bicycle?
  mai·*pee*·tahkh   ¿Maypitaq
  wee·see·kee·lee·*tah*·tah   wisikilitata
  ahl·kee·lai·*rui*·man?   alkilarquyman?
How much is it per hour/day?
  hai·*k'ah*·tahkh *kwees*·tahn   ¿Hayk'ataq kwistan
  sah·pah oo·rah/*p'oon*chai?   sapa ura/p'unchay?
Where can I buy a bike?
  mai·*pee*·tahkh   ¿Maypitaq
  wee·see·kee·lee·*tah*·tah   wisikilitata
  rahn·tee·*rui*·mahn?   rantirquyman?
I have a flat tyre.
  wee·see·kee·lee·*tai*·pah   Wisikilitaypa llantanmi
  lyahn·*tahn*·mee t'o·*ko*·ron   t'uqurqun.
Could you help me please?
  ah·*lyee*·choo   ¿Allichu
  yah·nah·pah·yoo·wahn·   yanapayuwa-
  kee·*mahn*·choo?   nkimanchu?

bicycle	wee·see·kee·*lee*·tah	*wisikilita*
puncture	*t'o*·ko	*t'uqu*
seat	tee·*yah*·nah	*tiyana*
tyre(s)	lyahn·tah(*koo*·nah)	*llanta(kuna)*

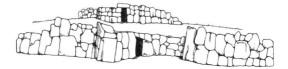

QURPACHANA
ACCOMMODATION

Accommodation choices range from luxury hotels in the larger cities and popular tourist towns, to a humble sleeping space with a rural Andean family. In the smaller communities, a few words of Quechua might be the secret to a comfortable night's sleep.

FINDING ACCOMMODATION
QURPACHANATA MASKHAY

I'm looking for (a) ...	...·tah mahs·k·hah·*shah*·nee	...-*ta* *maskhashani.*
accommodation	kor·pah·*chah*·nah	*qurpachana*
camping ground	*kahr*·pah	*karpa*
	roo·wah·*nah*·pahkh	*ruwanapaq*
	pahm·pah	*pampa*
boarding house/ hotel	kor·pah *wah*·see	*qurpa wasi*
Where's a/the ... hotel?	mai·*pee*·tahkh ... kor·pah *wah*·see kahn?	¿*Maypitaq* ... *qurpa wasi kan?*
best	lyoo·*mahn*·tah *ahn*·chah soo·mahkh	*lliwmanta* *ancha sumaq*
cheap	*mah*·nah chah·*nee*·yohk	*mana* *chaniyuq*
cheapest	lyoo·*mahn*·tah *pee*·see chah·*nee*·yok	*lliwmanta* *pisi* *chaniyuq*
clean	pee·*chahs*·kah	*pichasqa*
good	*ah*·lyeen	*allin*

ACCOMMODATION

Is there a hotel here?
   kahn·choo kor·pah
   wah·see *kai*·pee?   *¿Kanchu qurpa*
                                      wasi kaypi?

Is that a good hotel?
   ah·lyeen kor·pah
   wah·*see*·choo *chai*·kah?   *¿Allin qurpa*
                                      wasichu chayqa?

Is that a clean hotel?
   lui·*loo*·choo chai kor·pah
   wah·*see*·kah?   *¿Luyluchu chay qurpa*
                                      wasiqa?

Is that hotel nearby/far?
   sees·pah·lyah·*pee*·choo/
   kah·roo·*pee*·choo kah·shahn
   chai kor·pah wah·*see*·kah?   *¿Sispallapichu/*
                                      Karupichu kashan
                                      chay qurpa wasiqa?

Could you show me
that hotel, please?
   rekh·see·chee·wahn·kee·
   mahn·choo chai kor·pah
   wah·see·*tah*·kah?   *¿Riqsichiwanki·*
                                      manchu chay qurpa
                                      wasitaqa?

REQUESTS & QUERIES   MAÑAKUYKUNAPAS TAPUYKUNAPAS

Where can I sleep?
   mai·*pee*·tahkh poo·*nyoo*·man?   *¿Maypitaq puñuyman?*

Is there a toilet here?
   kahn·choo hees·p'ah·*koo*·nah/
   ees·koo·*sah*·roo kai·pee?   *¿Kanchu hisp'akuna/*
                                        iskusaru kaypi?

Where can I take a bath?
   mai·*pee*·tahkh
   ahr·mah·*kui*·mahn?   *¿Maypitaq*
                                        armakuyman?

WATER ...

There are two different words for 'water': *unu*, *oo*·*noo*, and *yaku*, *yah*·*koo*. The latter is used throughout the Andes.

Is there water to wash myself?
kahn·choo oo·nool/yah·koo
mahkh·ch·hee·koo·nai·pahkh?

¿Kanchu unu/yaku
maqchhikunaypaq?

Is there water to wash my face?
kahn·choo oo·nool/yah·koo
oo·p·hah·koo·nai·pahkh?

¿Kanchu unu/yaku
uphakunaypaq?

Could you please heat up
some water for me?
ah·lyee·choo oo·noo·tah/
yah·koo·tah
k'o·nyee·chee·poo·wahn·
kee·mahn·choo?

¿Allichu unuta/
yakuta
q'uñichipuwa-
nkimanchu?

Where can I wash my clothes?
mai·pee·tahkh
p'ah·chai·koo·nah·tah
t'ahkh·sah·rui·mahn?

¿Maypitaq
p'achaykunata
t'aqsaruyman?

Where's the river/spring?
mai·pee·tahkh mah·yool/
pookh·yoo kahn?

¿Maypitaq mayul/
pukyu kan?

Where can I find drinking water?
mai·pee·tahkh ook·yah·nah
oo·noo·tah tah·ree·rui·mahn?

¿Maypitaq ukyana
unuta tarirquyman?

Is there clean water here?
kahn·choo ch'oo·yah oo·nool/
yah·koo kai·pee?

¿Kanchu ch'uya unu/
yaku kaypi?

AROUND THE HOME

Remember that Andean houses may not have the
luxury of running water or indoor toilets. Be sure to
bring all of your own toiletries, and simply ask for a
tub for washing.

At meal times, your host family will expect you to
share in their food and conversation, and to try the
different dishes on offer.

That was delicious!
soo·mahkh mee·k·hoo·nah!   ¡Sumaq mikhuna!

ACCOMMODATION

Is there anything to drink?
kahn·choo oo·kyah·nah·pahkh ee·mah·lyah·pahs?
¿Kanchu ukyanapaq imallapas?

May I have some herbal tea?
pahkh·tah ko·rah oo·noo·tah/yah·koo·tah ko·wahn·kee·mahn?
¿Paqta qura unuta/yakuta quwankiman?

Is there anything to eat?
kahn·choo mee·k·hoo·nah·pahkh ee·mah·lyah·pahs?
¿Kanchu mikhunapaq imallapas?

What time do you want us to get up?
ee·mah oo·rahs·mee hah·tah·ree·koo·mahn?
¿Ima urasmi hatariykuman?

Can I help you with something?
pahkh·tah ee·mah·lyah·tah·pees yah·nah·pai·kee·mahn?
¿Paqta imallatapis yanapaykiman?

Can I leave my backpack here until tonight/tomorrow?
sah·ke·mahn·choo too·tah·kah·mah/ pah·kah·reen·kah·mah k'e·pee·tah kai·pee?
¿Saqiymanchu tutakama/ paqarinkama q'ipiyta kaypi?

May I leave my luggage here with you?
pahkh·tah mah·lee·tai·tah sah·ke·yoo·kui·kee·mahn?
¿Paqta malitayta saqiyukuykiman?

Could you lend me (a) ...?	*pahkh·tah ...·tah mah·nyah·wahn·kee·mahn?*	*¿Paqta ...-ta mañawan-nkiman?*
blanket	*kah·tah/free·sah·rah*	*qata/phrisara*
bucket	*bahl·dee*	*baldi*
wash basin	*poo·roo·nyah*	*puruña*

COMPLAINTS

It's very ...	*ahn·chah ...·n*	*Ancha ...-n*
cold	*chee·ree*	*chiri*
dark	*too·tah*	*tuta*
noisy	*rokh·yah*	*ruqya*

This ... is not clean.	*mah·nahn kai ...·kah pee·chas·kah·choo*	*Manan kay ...-qa pichasqachu.*
bed	*poo·nyoo·nah*	*puñuna*
blanket	*kah·tah/free·sah·rah/ choo·see*	*qata/frisara/ chusi*
house	*wah·see*	*wasi*
pillow	*sow·nah*	*sawna*
room	*kwahr·too*	*kwartu*
towel	*ch'ah·kee·chee·koo·nah/ too·wah·lyah*	*ch'akichikuna/ tuwalla*

PIÑARIKUY

HOMESTAYS   QURPACHAKUYKUNA

Homestays are common in smaller communities. In some cases, you may be able to arrange one through a travel agent in the city, but if you're the adventurous sort, you can always trust your luck and try to find one yourself.

Where can I find a place to stay tonight?

mai·pee·tahkh poo·nyoo·pah·koo·rui·mahn?	*¿Maypitaq puñupakurquyman?*

Could I/we please spend the night in your house?

ah·lyee·choo poo·nyoo·pah·yoo· kui·kee·mahn·choo?;	*¿Allichu puñupayu- kuykimanchu?;*
ah·lyee·choo poo·nyoo·pah·yoo· kui·kee·koo·mahn·choo?	*¿Allichu puñupayu- kuykikumanchu?*

We have our own mattresses/ sleeping bags.

poo·nyui·nai·koo kahn·mee	*Puñunayku kanmi.*

ACCOMMODATION

How much do you charge for ...?	*hai·k'ahn kwees·tahn ...?*	¿Hayk'an kwistan ...?
each night	*sah·pah too·tah*	sapa tuta
each day	*sah·pah p'oon·chai*	sapa p'unchay
both of us	*ees·kai·nee·koo·pahkh*	iskayni-ykupaq

Thank you, I'd like to stay
in your house.

sool·*pai*·kee, wah·*see·kee*·pee
kor·pah·*chai*·tahn
moo·*nai*·mahn

*Sulpayki, wasiykipi
qurpachaytan
munayman.*

THEY MAY SAY ...

ah·*lyeen*·mee, pah·sai·*kah*·mui
tai·*tai*/mah·*mai*
    That's OK. Come in sir/madam.

pahm·pah·chah·*yoo*·wai *mah*·nahn
poo·nyoo·*nai*·koo kahn·choo
    I'm sorry, but we don't have the room.

pahm·pah·chah·*yoo*·wai *mah*·nah
roo·nah·koo·*nah*·tah
qor·pah·chah·chee·*koo*·choo
    I'm sorry, but we don't take guests.

mai·ken·nee·kee·koo·nahn
qor·pah·chah·koon·*kee*·chees *kai*·pee?
    How many of you would like to stay?

hai·k'ah *too*·tahn poo·nyoo·pah·koon·*kee*·chees?
    How many nights?

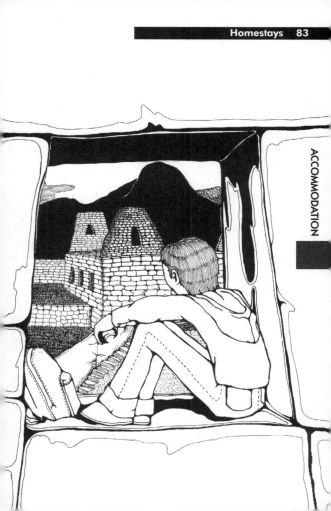

ACCOMMODATION

DEPARTURE

LLUQSIY

I'm/We're leaving now.
koo·*nahm*·kah
ree·poo·koo·*sahkh*·nyah/
ree·poo·koo·sahkh·*koo*·nyah

*Kunanqa
ripukusaqña/
ripukusaqkuña.*

Thank you for all your help.
sool·*pai* yah·nah·pah·wahs·
kai·kee·*mahn*·tah

*Sulpáy yanapawa-
sqaykimanta.*

Thank you for letting me stay
in your house.
sool·*pai* wah·see·*kee*·pee
kor·pah·chah·chee·wahs·
kai·kee·*mahn*·tah/
poo·nyoo·chee·wahs·
kai·kee·*mahn*·tah

*Sulpáy wasiykipi
qurpachachiwas
qaykimanta/
puñuchiwa-
sqaykimanta.*

I hope I can return someday.
ee·*chah*·pahs hai·*k'ahkh*·pahs
koo·tee·*mui*·mahn

*lchapas hayk'aqpas
kutimuyman.*

It was great staying at your place.
seen·*chee*·tah koo·see·*koo*·nee
wah·see·*kee*·pee
kor·pah·chah·chee·wahs·
kai·kee·*mahn*·tah

*Sinchita kusikuni
wasiykipi
qurpachachiwa-
sqaykimanta.*

How much do I owe you?
hai·*k'ah*·tahkh mah·noo·*kui*·kee?

¿Hayk'ataq manukuyki?

Here's payment for my stay.
kai kol·*ke*·tah koi·koo·*sai*·kee
wah·see·*kee*·pee
kor·pah·chah·chee·wahs·
kai·kee·*mahn*·tah

*Kay qulqita quykusayki
wasiykipi
qurpachachiwas-
qaykimanta.*

LLAQTAPI PURIY
AROUND TOWN

In some villages, Quechua will come in handy at archaeological tourist sites and in shops with Quechua names. Many of the typical nightlife activities and other forms of cosmopolitan entertainment in the larger Andean cities will be organised in Spanish or even in English. Signs will be in Spanish rather than Quechua.

LOOKING FOR ...   ... MASKHAY

Where's a/the ...?	mah·pee·tahkh	¿Mapitaq
	... kahn?	... kan?
bank	kol·keh wah·see	qulqi wasi
hotel	kor·pah wah·see	qurpa wasi
main square	plah·sah	plasa
market	k·hah·too	qhatu
police station	wahr·dee·yah	wardiya
post office	koo·ree·yoo	kuriyu
public toilet	hees·p'ah·koo·nah/	hisp'akuna/
	bah·nyoo	bañu
telephone	tee·lee·foo·noo·yokh	tiliphunuyuq
centre	wah·see	wasi
local authorities'	kah·mah·chekh·	kamachiq-
office (similar	koo·nahkh	kunaq
to a town hall)	wah·seen	wasin

TELECOMMUNICATIONS

IMAYMANA WILLACHIKUYKUNA

Is there a/an ...	*kahn*·choo ...	*¿Kanchu ...*
in this village?	kai lyahkh·*tah*·pee?	*kay llaqtapi?*
computer	koom·poo·tah·*roo*·rah	*kumputarura*
Internet service	een·*teer*·neet	*Intirnit*
telephone	tee·lee·*foo*·noo	*tiliphunu*

It's urgent!
 oos·k·hai·*pahkh*·mee!;   *¡Usqhaypaqmi!;*
 pree·see·sahkh·*pahkh*·mee!   *¡Prisisaqpaqmi!*

Making a Call

Tiliphunuwan Rimay

Hello.
 nah·pai·koo·*lyai*·kee.   *Napaykullayki.*
This is ... speaking.
 ...·n/·mee *kah*·nee   *...-n/-mi kani.*
I'd like to speak to ...
 ...·*wahn*·mee ree·*mai*·tah   *...-wanmi rimayta*
 moo·*nah*·nee   *munani.*
Who's calling?
 pee·*tahkh kahn*·kee?   *¿Pitaq kanki?*
Please tell ... I called.
 ah·*lyee*·choo ...·mahn   *Allichu ...-man*
 wee·lyah·poo·*wahn*·kee   *willapuwanki*
 tee·lee·foo·*noo*·pee   *tiliphunupi*
 wahkh·yah·moos·*kai*·tah   *waqyamusqayta.*

SIGHTSEEING   TURISTAKUNA PURISQAN

Where's the tourist office?
mai·*pee*·tahkh
too·rees·tah·koo·*nah*·pahkh
oo·fee·*see*·nah *kah*·shahn?

¿*Maypitaq*
turistakunapaq
ufisina kashan?

What are the opening hours?
ee·mah oo·*rahs*·mee
kee·chah·*koon*·pees
wees·k'ah·*koon*·pees?

¿*Ima urasmi*
kichakunpis
wisq'akunpis?

How much is the entry fee?
hai·k'ahn *kwees*·tahn
yai·koo·*nah*·pahkh?

¿*Hayk'an kwistan*
yaykunapaq?

I'd like to see (Machu Picchu).
(*mah*·choo *peek*·choo)·tah
k·hah·*wai*·tah/rekh·*see*·tah
moo·*nai*·mahn

(*Machu Pikchu*)-*ta*
qhawayta/riqsiyta
munayman.

Can we take photographs here?
foo·too·koo·*nah*·tah
kor·koi·koo·*mahm*·choo
kai·pee?

¿*Phutukunata*
qurquykumanchu
kaypi?

Could we take photographs of you?
ah·*lyee*·choo foo·*too*·tah
kor·kor·koi·kee·*mahn*·choo?

¿*Allichu phututa*
qurqurquykimanchu?

Could you take a photograph of me?
ah·*lyee*·choo foo·*too*·tah
kor·kor·ko·wahn·
kee·*mahn*·choo?

¿*Allichu phututa*
qurqurquwan-
kimanchu?

I'll send you the photographs.
foo·too·koo·*nah*·tah
ah·pah·chee·moo·*sai*·kee

Phutukunata
apachimusayki.

It's ...	...·n/·mee	...-*n/-mi.*
beautiful	*soo*·mahkh	*sumaq*
impressive	*koo*·sah *koo*·sah	*kusa kusa*
interesting	*seen*·chee ah·*lyeen*	*sinchi allin*
strange	hokh *rek*·ch'ahkh	*huq rikch'aq*

The Sights   Sumaq K'itikuna

What's that (building)?
  ee·*mah*·tahkh chai　　　　　*¿Imataq chay*
  (*hah*·toon wah·*se*·kah)?　　*(hatun wasiqa)?*
How old is that (building)?
  hai·k'ah wah·tah·*yokh*·mee　*¿Hayk'a watayuqmi*
  chai (*hah*·toon wah·*se*·kah)?　*chay hatun wasiqa?*

aqueduct	*yahr*·k-hah	yarqha
archaeological	t-hoo·*nees*·kahkh *nyow*·pah	thunisqa ñawpa
site	wah·see·*koo*·nah	wasikuna
burial site	*chooly*·pah	chullpa
cathedral	*hah*·toon een·*lee*·sah	hatun inlisa
church	een·*lee*·sah	inlisa
cave	*mah*·ch'ai	mach'ay
cemetery	*ah*·yah pahm·*pah*·nah	aya pampana
central plaza	*hah*·toon *plah*·sah	hatun plasa
ceremonial	*een*·kahkh	Inkaq
baths	ahr·mah·*koo*·nahn	armakunan
crowded	*ahs*·k-hah	askha
	roo·nah·*koo*·nah	runakuna
dance	*too*·sui	tusuy
doorway	hai·*koo*·nah *poon*·koo	haykuna punku
festival	*rai*·mee	raymi
fortress	poo·*kah*·rah	pukara
gate	*hah*·toon *poon*·koo	hatun punku
Inca trail	*een*·kah poo·*rees*·kahn	Inka purisqan
	nyahn	ñan
monastery	*ahk*·lyah *wah*·see;	aklla wasi;
	moo·nahs·tee·*ree*·yoo	munastiriyu
museum	moo·*see*·yoo	musiyu
niche	*oos*·nool/t'*o*·ko	usnu/t'uqu
offering	hai·wah·*ree*·kui	haywarikuy
park	pook·*lyah*·nah *pahm*·pah;	pukllana pampa;
	pahr·kee	parki

principal temple	*hah*·toon *mahn*·kos *wah*·see	hatun manqus wasi
royal palace	*kees*·wahr/*hah*·toon *kahn*·chah	kiswar/hatun kancha
royal tomb	*chooly*·pah	chullpa
ruins	*rah*·kai *rah*·kai; t-hoo·*nees*·kah wah·see·*koo*·nah	raqay raqay; thunisqa wasikuna
settlement	*lyahkh*·tah/*ai*·lyoo	llaqta/ayllu
statue	*reek*·ch'ai/ ees·tah·*too*·wah	rikch'ay/ istatuwa
temple	*mahn*·kos *wah*·see	manqus wasi
temple of the Sun	ko·ree·*kahn*·chah	Qurikancha
textile/weaving	*ah*·wah	awa
volcano	*nee*·nah p-*hokh*·chekh *or*·ko	nina phuqchiq urqu
warrior	*ow*·kah *poo*·rekh	awqa puriq
window	k-hah·wah·*ree*·nah/*t'o*·ko	qhawarina/t'uqu

AROUND TOWN

Tours   Turistakuna Purinan

How much is a guide?
hai·*k'ah*·tahkh *koob*·rahn
poo·sai·*kah*·chahkh *roo*·nah?

*¿Hayk'ataq kubran
pusaykachaq runa?*

Could we hire an English-speaking/
Spanish-speaking guide?
meen·*k'ah*·kui·koo·*mahn*·choo
een·lees/kahs·tee·*lyah*·noo
ree·mahkh poo·sai·kah·*chahkh*·tah?

*¿Mink'akuykumanchu
inlis/kastillanu
rimaq pusaykachaqta?*

I'm with them.
pai·koo·nah·*wahn*·mee
kah·*shah*·nee

*Paykunawanmi
kashani.*

I've lost my group.
too·rees·tah·mah·see·koo·*nah*·tahn
cheen·kah·chee·koor·*ko*·nee

*Turistamasikunatan
chinkachikurquni.*

Have you seen a group of foreigners?
k·hah·wahr·kahn·*kee*·choo
hah·wah roo·nah·koo·*nah*·tah?

*¿Qhawarqankichu
hawa runakunata?*

YOU SAY POTATO ...

Historically, there have been more than 80 distinct ways of writing the name of the Quechua language. This was due mostly to variations in regional pronunciations, and also to a misanalysis of the relationship between different sounds. Some examples: *cjeswa, kechwa, khetsua, kichwa, kkechuwa, keshua, keswa, qheswa, q'eswa, qhexwa, quichua* and *qqichua*. In modern times, with the increasing standardisation of the Quechua alphabet, some researchers have proposed the following spellings: *kichwa, qhiswa* and *qichwa*.

GOING OUT

MAYTAPAS RIY

'Going out' in smaller communities is generally limited to visiting neighbours or attending local festivities.

This place is great.
kai lyahkh·*tah*·kah/fees·*tah*·kah seen·chee soo·*mahkh*·mee

Kay llaqtaqa/phistaqa sinchi sumaqmi.

I'm having a good time here.
k'o·choo·ree·koo·*shah*·neen *kai*·pee

Q'uchurikushanin kaypi.

Shall we go somewhere else?
***pahkh*·tah mai·*tah*·pahs reen·*chees*·mahn?**

¿Paqta maytapas rinchisman?

I'm sorry, I'm a terrible dancer.
dees·peen·sah·*yoo*·wai, *mah*·nahn koo·*sah*·tah too·soo·*nee*·choo

Dispinsayuway, manan kusata tusunichu.

Where to Go

Maytan Rinkiman

What's there to do in the evenings?
ee·mah·*tah*·tahkh roo·nah·*koo*·nah too·*tah*·pee roo·*wahn*·koo k'o·choo·ree·koo·nahn·*koo*·pahkh?

¿Imatataq runakuna tutapi ruwanku q'uchurikunankupaq?

What shall we do tonight?
ee·mah·*tah*·tahkh roo·wahn·*chees*·mahn *koo*·nahn too·*tah*?

¿Imatataq ruwanchisman kunan tuta?

Are there musicians?
***kahn*·choo moo·see·koo·*koo*·nah?**

¿Kanchu musikukuna?

AROUND TOWN

I feel like going to a/the ...	...man ree·tah moo·nai·mahn	...-man riyta munayman.
chicha bar	ah·k-hah wah·see	aqha wasi
local fiesta	kai lyahkh·tah·pee fees·tah	kay llaqtapi phista
restaurant	mee·k-hoo·nah wah·see	mikhuna wasi

I'd like to ...	...tah moo·nai·mahn	...-ta munayman.
dance	too·sui	tusuy
drink coffee/ tea	kah·fee/ tee·tah ook·yai	kaphiy/ tiyta ukyay
walk	poo·ree	puriy

Invitations

Inwitasiyunkuna

What are you doing this evening?
ee·mah·tah·tahkh koo·nahn
too·tah roo·wahn·kee?

¿Imatataq kunan
tuta ruwanki?

Would you like to go out
somewhere today/tomorrow?
mai·tah·pahs ree·tah
moo·nahn·kee·mahn·choo
koo·nahn/pah·kah·reen?

¿Maytapas riyta
munankimanchu
kunan/paqarin?

Would you like to go for a drink?
ee·mah·lyah·tah·pees
ook·yah·nah·pahkh
mai·tah·pees ree·tah
moo·nahn·kee·mahn·choo?

¿Imallatapis
ukyanapaq
maytapis riyta
munankimanchu?

Would you like to go for a meal?
ee·mah·lyah·tah·pees
mee·k-hoo·nah·pahkh
mai·tah·pees ree·tah
moo·nahn·kee·mahn·choo?

¿Imallatapis
mikhunapaq
maytapis riyta
munankimanchu?

Do you know a good restaurant?
rekh·seen·kee·choo
hokh soo·makh
mee·k-hoo·nah wah·see·tah?

¿Riqsinkichu
huq sumaq
mikhuna wasita?

My shout/treat. (I'll buy)
> *no·*kahn een·wee·tah·*sai·*kee   *Nuqan inwitasayki.*

Do you want to go to the ...?
> ...tah *ree·*tah   *¿...-ta riyta*
> moo·nahn·*kee·*choo?   *munankichu?*

Come on!/Let's go!
> *hah·*koo!/hah·*koo·*chee!   *¡Haku!/¡Hakuchi!*

Responding to Invitations
Inwitasiyunkunata Kutichiy

Sure!
> ah·*lyeen·*mee!   *¡Allinmi!*

Yes, I'd love to.
> ah·*ree,* moo·nai·*mahn·*mee   *Arí, munaymanmi.*

Yes. Where shall we go?
> ah·*ree.* mai·*tah·*tahkh   *Arí. ¿Maytataq*
> reen·*chees·*mahn?   *rinchisman?*

No. I'm afraid I can't.
> *mah·*nahn ree·tah   *Manan riyta*
> ah·tee·*nee·*choo   *atinichu.*

I don't have time.
> *mah·*nahn *teem·*pui *kahn·*choo   *Manan timpuy kanchu.*

What about tomorrow?
> ee·mah·*tah·*tahkh roo·*wahn·*kee   *¿Imatataq ruwanki*
> pah·*kah·*reen?   *paqarin?*

Arranging to Meet
Tinkunapaq Rimanakuy

What time shall we meet?
> *ee·*mah oo·*rahs·*mee   *¿Ima urasmi*
> teen·koo·*soon·*chees?   *tinkusunchis?*

Where shall we meet?
> mai·*peen* teen·koo·*soon·*chees?   *¿Maypin tinkusunchis?*

Let's meet (at eight o'clock) at the ...
> (lahs *oo·*choo oo·*rahs·*tah)   *(Las uchu urasta)*
> teen·*koo·*soon ...pee   *Tinkusun ...-pi.*

OK. I'll see you then.
   koo·sah
   too·pahn·ahn·chees·*kah*·mah

Kusa.
Tupananchiskama.

Agreed!/OK!
   ah·*lyeen*·mee!/*koo*·sah!

¡Allinmi!/¡Kusa!

I'll come over at (six/eight) o'clock.
   (lahs *sah*·yees/lahs *oo*·choo)
   oo·*rahs*·tah hah·*moo*·sahkh

(Las sayis/Las uchu)
Urasta hamusaq.

I'll try to make it.
   ah·*tees*·pah *mah*·nah
   ah·tees·*pah*·pees
   hah·moo·*sahkh*·mee

Atispa mana
atispapis
hamusaqmi.

I'll be along later.
   ahs·wahn k·he·pah·tah·*rahkh*·mee
   hah·*moo*·sahkh

Aswan qhipataraqmi
hamusaq.

Where will you be?
   mai·peen *kahn*·kee?

¿Maypin kanki?

See you later/tomorrow.
   too·pah·nahn·chees·*kah*·mah/
   pah·kah·reen·*kah*·mah

Tupananchiskama/
Paqarinkama.

Sorry I'm late.
   pahm·pah·chah·*yoo*·wai
   k·he·pah·ree·koos·khai·*mahn*·tah

Pampachayuway
qhiparikusqaymanta.

FAMILY

The family is the highest priority for every individual in Andean society. Extended families are the norm, with parents, children, grandparents and sometimes other relatives living together. Kinship often extends beyond the biological family through marriage and a system where godparents are expected to act as a second set of parents to a child. The more children you have, the more godparents, and thus the larger the extended family and community, known as an *ayllu, ai·lyoo*.

Romantic relationships, marital status and children are common topics of conversation for young people.

QUESTIONS & ANSWERS

TAPUYKUNAPIS KUTICHIYKUNAPIS

Are you married? (asked to a woman)

| ko·sah·*yokh*·choo/ | ¿Qusayuqchu/ |
| kah·sah·*roo*·choo *kahn*·kee? | Kasaruchu kanki? |

Are you married? (asked to a man)

| wahr·mee·*yokh*·choo/ | ¿Warmiyuqchu/ |
| kah·sah·*roo*·choo *kahn*·kee? | Kasaruchu kanki? |

I'm (a) ...	*no*·kah ...n/·mee *kah*·nee	Nuqa ...-n/-mi kani.
divorced	t'ah·qah·nah·*koos*·kah/ t'ah·*kahs*·kah	t'aqanakusqa/ t'aqasqa
married (f)	ko·*sah*·yokh	qusayuq
married (m)	wahr·*mee*·yokh	warmiyuq
separated	t'ah·*kahs*·kah	t'aqasqa
single (f)	sool·*tee*·rah; *mah*·nah ko·*sah*·yokh	sultira; mana qusayuq
single (m)	sool·*tee*·roo; *mah*·nah wahr·*mee*·yokh	sultiru; mana warmiyuq
widow	*wahr*·mee *sah*·pah	warmi sapa
widower	*sah*·pahn k·*hah*·ree	sapan qhari

I have a partner.
> yah·nah·*yokh*·mee *kah*·nee   *Yanayuqmi kani.*

We live together
but we're not married.
> no·*kai*·koo koos·*kai*·koon   *Nuqayku kuskaykun*
> tee·*yai*·koo,   *tiyayku,*
> ee·*chah*·kah *mah*·nahn   *ichaqa manan*
> kah·sah·rah·koos·*kah*·choo *kai*·koo *kasarakusqachu kayku.*

The word 'child' isn't used by men, who must always specify the sex of their children. Women, however, can be asked or might say these phrases:

How many ...	*hai*·k'ahn ...?	*¿Hayk'an ...?*
do you have?		
children	wah·wai·kee·*koo*·nah	*wawaykikuna*
sons	k·*hah*·ree	*qhari*
	wah·wai·kee·*koo*·nah	*wawaykikuna*
daughters	*wahr*·mee	*warmi*
	wah·wai·kee·*koo*·nah	*wawaykikuna*

I don't have any children.
> *mah*·nahn wah·wai·*koo*·nai   *Manan wawaykunay.*

I have ... daughter(s)/son(s).
> ...n/·mee *wahr*·mee/k·*hah*·ree   *...-n/-mi warmi/qhari*
> wah·wai(*koo*·nah)   *waway(kuna).*

How many brothers/sisters
do you have?
> *hai*·k'ahn too·rai·kee·*koo*·nah/   *¿Hayk'an turaykikuna/*
> nyah·nyai·kee·*koo*·nah?   *ñañaykikuna?*

Men can be asked or might say these phrases:

How many ...	*hai*·k'ahn ...?	*¿Hayk'an ...?*
do you have?		
sons	choo·ree·*koo*·nah	*churiykuna*
daughters	oo·soo·see·kee·*koo*·nah	*ususiykikuna*

I don't have any sons/daughters.
*mah·*nahn *choo·*ree·*koo·*nah/
oo·soo·see·*koo·*nah *kahn·*choo

Manan churiykuna/
ususiykuna kanchu.

I have ... daughter(s)/son(s).
...·n/·mee *choo·*ree(*koo*·nah)/
oo·*soo·*see(*koo*·nah)

...-n/-mi churiy(kuna)/
ususiy(kuna).

How many brothers/sisters
do you have?
*hai·*k'ahn wow·*kay·*kee·*koo·*nah/
pah·*nai·*kee·*koo·*nah?

¿Hayk'an wawqiykikuna/
panaykikuna?

Both men and women can be asked or might say:

How old are they?
*hai·*k'ah wah·tah·*yokh·*mee
pai·*koo·*nah *kahn·*koo?

¿Hayk'a watayuqmi
paykuna kanku?

Do you live with your family?
ai·lyui·kee·*wahn·*choo/
fah·mee·lyai·kee·*wahn·*choo
tee·*yahn·*kee?

¿Aylluykiwanchu/
phamillaykiwanchu
tiyanki?

I live with my family.
ai·lyui·*wahn·*mee tee·*yah·*nee

Aylluywanmi tiyani.

Do you have a girlfriend/boyfriend?
yah·nah·*yokh·*choo *kahn·*kee?

¿Yanayuqchu kanki?

THE PERFECT ENDING

Remember, when using the *-n/-mi* suffix, choose
the *-n* ending when the preceding root word ends
in a vowel, and the *-mi* ending when it ends in
a consonant. Note that using the *-mi* ending
will change which syllable is stressed. This is a
general rule in this book.

FAMILY MEMBERS   AYLLUKUNA

aunt	*tee·*yah	*tiya*
baby	*wah·*wah/	*wawa/*
	wah·*wah·*chah	*wawacha*
boy	er·kel/*makh·*tah	*irqi/maqta*
boyfriend	*yah·*nah	*yana*
brother (of a woman)	*too·*rah/*too·*ree	*tura/turi*
brother (of a man)	wai·kel/*wow·*ke	*wayqi/wawqi*
child (of a woman)	*wah·*wah	*wawa*
daughter (of a woman)	*wahr·*mee *wah·*wah	*warmi wawa*
daughter (of a man)	oo·*soo·*see;	*ususi;*
	*wahr·*mee *choo·*ree	*warmi churi*
family	*ai·*lyoo/	*ayllu/*
	fah·*mee·*lyah	*phamilla*
father	tai·tah/*pah·*pah/	*tayta/papa/*
	*tah·*tah	*tata*
father-in-law	*sui·*roo	*suyru*
girl	*p'ahs·*nyah/*see·*pahs/	*p'asña/sipas/*
	see·*pahs·*chah	*sipascha*
girlfriend	*yah·*nah	*yana*
grandchild	*hah·*wai	*haway*
grandfather	*hah·*toon tai·tah	*hatun tayta*
	ah·*poo·*chah;	*apucha;*
	mah·*choo·*lah;	*machula;*
	hah·*too·*koo;	*hatuku;*
	ah·*wee·*loo	*awilu*
grandmother	*hah·*toon *mah·*mah;	*hatun mama;*
	ah·*wee·*lah	*awila*
husband	*ko·*sah	*qusa*
mother	*mah·*mah	*mama*
mother-in-law	*sui·*rah	*suyra*
parents	tai·tah·*mah·*mah	*taytamama*
sister (of a woman)	*nyah·*nyah	*ñaña*
sister (of a man)	*pah·*nah/*pah·*nee	*pana/pani*
son (of a woman)	k-*hah·*ree *wah·*wah	*qhari wawa*

son (of a man)	*choo*·ree	*churi*
stepfather	*k-he*·pah *tai*·tah	*qhipa tayta*
stepmother	*k-he*·pah *mah*·mah	*qhipa mama*
uncle	*tee*·yoo	*tiyu*
wife	*wahr*·mee	*warmi*

TALKING WITH PARENTS

TAYTAMAMAKUNAWAN RIMAY

When's the baby due?
   hai·*k'ahkh*·mee
   wah·chah·*koon*·kee?

   ¿*Hayk'aqmi*
   wachakunki?

What are you going to call
your baby?
   ee·*mah*·tahkh wah·*wai*·kekh
   soo·teen *kahn*·kah?

   ¿*Imataq wawaykiq*
   sutin kanqa?

Women can be asked or might say these phrases:

Is this your first child?
   p-*hee*·wee
   wah·wai·*kee*·choo pai?

   ¿*Phiwi*
   wawaykichu pay?

How old are your children?
   hai·*k'ah* wah·tah·*yohkh*·mee
   wah·wai·kee·*koo*·nah?

   ¿*Hayk'a watayuqmi*
   wawaykikuna?

Men can be asked or might say:

How old are your sons/daughters?
   hai·*k'ah* wah·tah·*yohkh*·mee
   choo·ree·kee·*koo*·nah/
   oo·soo·see·kee·*koo*·nah?

   ¿*Hayk'a watayuqmi*
   churiykikuna/
   ususiykikuna?

FAMILY FAVOURS

Mutual cooperation among families and members of the *ayllu*, *ai·lyoo*, 'extended family', is a way of life. *Ayni*, *ai·nee*, 'reciprocal labour', assures that if you do someone a favour or lend them something today, they'll return the favour tomorrow. A similar concept is *mink'a*, *meen·k'ah*, which means 'cooperation' or 'collaboration'.

Incredible! You look so young!
    mah·nah ee·nyee·nah!   ¡Mana iñina!
    see·pahs/wai·nah   Sipas/Wayna
    hee·nah kah·shahn·kee   hina kashanki.

Does she/he attend school?
    yah·chai wah·see·tah reen·choo?   ¿Yachay wasita rinchu?

Who looks after the children?
    pee·tahkk   ¿Pitaq
    wahr·mah·chah·koo·nah·tah   warmachakunata
    k·hah·wahn?   qhawan?

Do you have grandchildren?
    hah·wai·kee·koo·nah kahn·choo?   ¿Hawaykikuna kanchu?

What's your baby's name?
    ee·mah·tahkh wah·wah·chai·kekh   ¿Imataq wawachaykiq
    soo·teen?   sutin?

Is it a boy or a girl?
    er·ke·choo ee·chah   ¿Irqichu icha
    p'ahs·nyah·choo?   p'asñachu?

Does she/he let you sleep at night?
    poo·nyoon·choo too·tah·pee?   ¿Puñunchu tutapi?

What a beautiful child!
    ee·mah soo·makh wah·wah!   ¡Ima sumaq wawa!

She/He looks like you.
    pai·kah kahn·mahn·mee   Payqa qanmanmi
    reekh·ch'ah·koon   rikch'akun.

TALKING WITH CHILDREN

WARMAKUNAWAN RIMAY

What's your name?
  ee·mahn soo·*tee*·kee?   *¿Iman sutiyki?*

How old are you?
  hai·k'ah wah·tah·chah·*yokh*·mee   *¿Hayk'a watachayuqmi*
  kahn·kee?   *kanki?*

When's your birthday?
  hai·*k'ahkh*·mee   *¿Hayk'aqmi*
  wah·t'a hoon·t'ai·*nee*·kee?   *wat'a hunt'ayniki?*

Do you have brothers and sisters?
(said to a girl)
  too·rah·nyah·nyah·*yokh*·choo   *¿Tura-ñañayuqchu*
  kahn·kee?   *kanki?*

Do you have brothers and sisters?
(said to a boy)
  wow·ke·pah·nah·*yokh*·choo   *¿Wawqi-panayuqchu*
  kahn·kee?   *kanki?*

Do you go to school?
  yah·chai wah·*see*·tah/   *¿Yachay wasita/*
  ees·kui·*lah*·tah reen·kee·choo?   *iskuylata rinkichu?*

Do you like school?
  moo·nahn·*kee*·choo *yah*·chai   *¿Munankichu yachay*
  wah·*see*·tah/ees·kui·*lah*·tah?   *wasita/iskuylata?*

Is your teacher nice?
  ah·lyeen roo·*nah*·choo   *¿Allin runachu*
  yah·chah·chekh·*nee*·kee?   *yachachiqniyki?*

Do you play soccer?
  pee·*loo*·tah hai·*t'ai*·tah   *¿Piluta hayt'ayta*
  pookh·*lyahn*·kee·choo?   *pukllankichu?*

What kind of games do you play?
  ee·mah   *¿Ima*
  pookh·*lyai*·koo·*nah*·tahn   *pukllaykunatan*
  pookh·*lyahn*·kee?   *pukllanki?*

Do you study English?
  een·lees see·*mee*·tah   *¿Inlis simita*
  yah·chahn·*kee*·choo?   *yachankichu?*

FAMILY

Do you want to play?
   pookh·*lyai*·tah
   moo·nahn·*kee*·choo?

¿Pukllayta
munankichu?

What shall we play?
   ee·mah·*tah*·tahkh
   pookh·lyahn·*chees*·mahn?

¿Imatataq
pukllanchisman?

Do you have a pet at home?
   chee·*tai*·kee *kahn*·choo
   wah·see·*kee*·pee?

¿Chitayki kanchu
wasiykipi?

MUNASQANCHISKUNAPAS RUWANANCHISKUNAPAS
INTERESTS & ACTIVITIES

Some activities that Westerners think of as hobbies, such as gardening, walking and cooking, are still very much a way of life for Andean people.

COMMON INTERESTS		KAQLLA MUNASQANCHISKUNA
What do you do in your spare time?		
	ee·mah·*tah*·tahkh roo·*wahn*·kee teem·*pui*·kee *kahkh*·teen?	¿Imatataq ruwanki timpuyki kaqtin?
Do you like ...?	...tah moo·nahn·*kee*·choo?	¿...-ta munankichu?
I like ...	...tah moo·*nah*·neen	...-ta munanin.
I don't like ...	*mah*·nahn ...tah moo·nah·*nee*·choo	Manan ...-ta munanichu.
cooking	*wai*·k'ui	wayk'uy
dancing	*too*·sui	tusuy
fishing	*chahly*·wai; chahly·*wah*·kui; *chahly*·wah *hah*·p'ee	challway; challwakuy; challwa hap'iy
food	mee·*k·hoo*·nah	mikhuna
getting together with friends	k·hoo·yah·nah·kokh· mah·see·koo·*nah*·wahn hoo·nyoo·*nah*·kui	khuyanakuq- masikunawan huñunakuy
hiking	*poo*·ree	puriy
hunting	*hah*·p'ee/*chah*·kui	hap'iy/chakuy
music	moo·*see*·kah	musika
reading	*lee*·yee/ nyah·*ween*·chai	liyiy/ ñawinchay
singing	*tah*·kee	takiy
talking	*ree*·mai	rimay

103

INTERESTS & ACTIVITIES

I make ...	...*tahn* roo·*wah*·nee	...-*tan ruwani*
clothes	p'ah·chah·*koo*·nah	*p'achakuna*
embroidery	*wel*·k'oy	*wilq'uy*
handicrafts	ahr·tee·sah·*nee*·yah	*artisaniya*
jewellery	ee·lyah/oo·*mee*·nyah	*illa/umiña*
pottery	*rakh*·ch'ee/*k'akh*·rah	*raqch'i/k'akra*
textiles	ah·wai·*koo*·nah	*awaykuna*
carve (only stone)	*koo*·chui/*ch'e*·koi	*kuchuy/ch'iquy*
draw	se·*ken*·chai	*siq'inchay*
embroider	*wel*·k'oy	*wilq'uy*
paint	*lyoo*·see/*peen*·tai	*llusiy/pintay*
sew	*see*·rai	*siray*
spin (thread or yarn)	*pooch*·kai/*poos*·kai	*puchkay/puskay*
weave	*ah*·wai	*away*

SPORT   PUKLLAYKUNA

What sport do you play?
ee·mah pookh·*lyai*·koo·*nah*·tahn pookh·*lyan*·kee?

¿Ima pukllaykunatan pukllanki?

I play soccer/volleyball.
[pee·*loo*·tah hai·*t'ai*·tah; boo·*lee*·tah] pookh·*lyah*·nee

[piluta hayt'ay-ta; bulita] pukllani.

I can swim.
wai·*t'ai*·tah yah·*chah*·nee

Wayt'ayta yachani.

I like to run.
pah·*wai*·tahn moo·*nah*·nee

Pawaytan munani.

I like fishing.
chahly·wah hah·*p'ee*·tahn moo·*nah*·nee

Challwa hap'itan munani.

I know how to bullfight.
too·roo pookh·*lyai*·tah yah·*chah*·nee

Turu pukllayta yachani.

Do you like sports?
   pook·lyai·koo·*nah*·tah
   moo·nahn·*kee*·choo?

*¿Pukllaykunata
munankichu?*

Yes, very much.
   ah·*ree*, ahn·*chah*·tahn
   moo·*nah*·nee

*Arí, anchatan
munani.*

No, not at all.
   mah·nahn moo·nah·*nee*·choo

Manan munanichu.

I like watching sport.
   k·hah·wai·*lyah*·tah moo·*nah*·nee

Qhawayllata munani.

Talking about Soccer

Piluta Hayt'aymanta Rimay

Do you follow soccer?
   pee·*loo*·tah hai·*t'ai*·tah
   pah·sahkh koo·*tee*·lyah
   k·hah·wahn·*kee*·choo?

*¿Piluta hayt'ayta
pasaq kutilla
qhawankichu?*

Which team do you support?
   mai·ken·*neen*·tahkh
   ee·kee·*pui*·kee?

*¿Mayqinnintaq
ikipuyki?*

Who's winning?
   mai·ken·*neen*·tahkh
   lyah·*lyee*·shahn?

*¿Mayqinnintaq
llallishan?*

Do you play in a team?
   ee·kee·*poo*·pee
   pookh·lyahn·*kee*·choo?

*¿Ikipupi
pukllankichu?*

Do you want to play soccer?
   pee·*loo*·tah hai·*t'ai*·tah
   moo·nahn·*kee*·choo?

*¿Piluta hayt'ayta
munankichu?*

THEY MAY YELL …

gool!	Goal!
pee·nahl!	Penalty!
ow·sai!	Offside!
tee·roo *lyoo*·ree!	Free kick!

MUSIC   *MUSIKA*

Traditional Andean music takes a variety of forms. The best known include the *waynu*, **wai·**noo, which can be fast or slow, happy or sad; the *harawi*, hah·**rah·**wee, typically a sweet but sad song; the *waylas*, **wai·**lahs, a fast melody; and the *sikuri*, see·**koo·**ree, which starts out slowly but gradually increases in tempo. It's often used to express Andean spiritual tradition and is popular in worship ceremonies. Each style of music is performed using distinctive instruments, and has its own dance variations.

The *cumbia*, **koom·**bya, is popular throughout the Andes, as is the *chicha*, **chee·**chah, genre: a mixture of coastal *cumbia* and the *waynu* (not to be confused with the popular drink *chicha*).

RATTLE AND HUM

Since pre-Columbian times, the instruments of the Andes have included various types of panpipes, flutes, drums, a guitar-like instrument made from an armadillo shell and leg rattles made of pig or goat hooves. In modern times, guitars, violins and harps have been added to the traditional repertoire of instruments, encouraging innovation in the styles and rhythms of Andean music.

Generally, Quechua speakers are very pleased to talk about music and instruments, as they have profound meaning in their lives.

antara/rundadur   ahn·**tah·**rah/roon·**dah·**door
    panpipe of bamboo, with a single row of pipes.
    It's called a *rundadur* in Ecuador only.
chaqchas/chullus   chahkh·chahs/choo·**lyoos**
    Bolivian leg rattle, made of ribbon with goat or pig
    hooves woven onto it

RATTLE AND HUM (cont.)

charangu/kirkinchu   chah·*rahn*·goo/
keer·*keen*·choo
small Andean ten-string guitar, made of armadillo shell or carved wood

harpa   hahr·pah
harp

kañari/   kah·*nyah*·ree/
waqraphuku   wahkh·rah·*p*-hoo·koo
Andean horn, made from a cow's horn

pinkuyllu   peen·*kui*·lyoo
Andean long flute, made from hardwood

pututu   poo·*too*·too
conch shell horn

qina   ke·nah
Andean flute, made from bone or hardwood

siku   see·koo
panpipe of cane or bamboo, with two rows of pipes

tinya   teen·yah
tambourine or small drum, made from tree bark and goat skin

ukarina   oo·kah·*ree*·nah
Andean globular flute

wankar   wahn·kahr
mid-sized Andean drum of sheep skin

wankara   wahn·*kah*·rah
large, round Andean drum, made of wood, shell and goat skin

waylachu   wai·*lah*·choo
devil *charango*; has metal strings that produce a sharp sound

wiyulin   wee·*yoo*·leen
violin or fiddle

INTERESTS & ACTIVITIES

Do you like ...?	...tah moo·nahn·*kee*·choo?	¿...-ta munankichu?
listening to music	moo·see·*kah*·tah oo·*yah*·ree	musikata uyariy
dancing	*too*·sui	tusuy

Do you know how to play ...?
...tah wah·kah·cheen·*kee*·choo? ¿...-ta waqachinkichu?
I play ...
...tah wah·kah·*chee*·nee ...-ta waqachini.
Where can I hear traditional music around here?
mai·*pee*·tahkh
see·koo·ree·koo·*nah*·tah
oo·*yah*·reer·*koi*·mahn kai
lyahkh·*tah*·pee?

¿Maypitaq
sikurikunata
uyarirquyman kay
llaqtapi?

TALKING ABOUT TRAVELLING

PURIYMANTA RIMAY

I've been travelling for (two) months.
  (ees·kai) kee·*lyah*·nyahn
  poo·*ree*·lyah poo·ree·*koo*·nee

*(Iskay) killañan
purilla purikuni.*

I'm going to ...
  ...·*sahkh*·mee

...-saqmi.

I've been to ...
  ...·pee poo·ree·*moor*·*kah*·nee

...-pi purimurqani.

Is it safe for women travellers
on their own?
  ah·*leen*·choo sah·pah·*lyahn*·koo
  wahr·mee·*koo*·nah *chai*·pee
  poo·ree·moo·*nahn*·koo·pahkh?

*¿Allinchu sapallanku
warmikuna chaypi
purimunankupaq?*

I thought	...·ch/·chah chai	...-ch/-cha chay
it was ...	*nees*·pah *nee*·nee	*nispa nini.*
boring	*mah*·nah ah·*lyeen*	*mana allin*
great	ee·*mah soo*·mahkh	*ima sumaq*
horrible	*mee*·lyai	*millay*
OK	*koo*·sah	*kusa*
too expensive	*ahn*·chah chah·*nee*·yokh	*ancha chaniyuq*

STAYING IN TOUCH

ATUNAKUKUY

Tomorrow is my last day here.
  pah·*kah*·reen·kah·*mah*·lyahn
  kai·pee *kah*·sahkh

*Paqarinkamallan
kaypi kasaq.*

Let's swap addresses.
  dee·*reek*·see·*yoon*·neen·*chees*·tah
  koi·*koo*·nah·koo·*soon*·*yah*

*Diriksiyunninchista
quykunakusunyá.*

I'll send you copies of the photos.
  foo·too·*koo*·nahkh
  koo·pee·*yahn*·tah
  ah·pah·chee·moo·*sai*·keen

*Phutukunaq
kupiyanta
apachimusaykin.*

I'll write to you.
  kel·kah·moo·*sai*·keen

Qilqamusaykin.

It's been great meeting you.
 ahn·*chah*·tahn koo·see·*koo*·nee
 rekh·see·koos·*pai*·kee

*Anchatan kusikuni
riqsikuspayki.*

Keep in touch!
 kel·kah·nah·koo·soon·*yah*!/
 wah·too·nah·koo·koo·soon·*yah*!

*¡Qilqanakusunyá!/
¡Watunakukusunyá!*

PUTTING THE RECORD STRAIGHT

The early colonial period (1532–1820s) produced two
important literary works by *misti,* **mees-tee,** mixed-
blood authors, still well known today.

*The Royal Commentaries of the Incas and General
History of Peru* (1609), by Garcilaso de la Vega,
compares the greatness of the Inca civilization with
the great classical civilizations of Western history. The
author, the son of an Inca princess and a Spanish
conquistador, felt the need to validate his indigenous
heritage through comparison with his Spanish roots.
While the work is in Spanish, it's main thrust is to glorify
the Inca empire, putting it on par with the Roman empire
that gave rise to the Spanish empire.

The second work is *New Chronicle and Good
Government* (1615), by Felipe Guaman Poma de Ayala.
His 1300-page letter to the Spanish king is written
in a complex combination of Spanish and Quechua,
interspersed with other indigenous languages. He offers
anecdotes from indigenous life before the conquest, to
illustrate how poorly the King's representatives in the
New World were faring in their administrative tasks.

TREKKING

Wilderness adventures and trekking are excellent ways to explore some of the more remote communities and archaeological sites. Companies based in highland cities specialise in arranging treks and mountain climbing expeditions. The local guides and porters often speak Quechua.

GETTING INFORMATION   TAPUKUY

Where can I find out about
hiking trails in the region?
    pee·*tah*·tahkh tah·*pui*·mahn
    kai lyahkh·*tah*·pee poo·*ree*·nah
    nyahn·koo·nah·*mahn*·tah?

        ¿Pitataq tapuyman
        kay llaqtapi purina
        ñankunamanta?

Who knows the hiking trails?
    pee·tahkh poo·*ree*·nah
    nyahn·koo·*nah*·tah rekh·seen?

        ¿Pitaq purina
        ñankunata riqsin?

Do we need a guide?
    moo·nai·koo·*mahn*·choo
    nyahn rekh·see·*chekh*·tah?

        ¿Munaykumanchu
        ñan riqsichiqta?

Are there guided treks here?
    kahm·choo nyahn
    rekh·see·chekh·*koo*·nah *kai*·pee?

        ¿Kanchu ñan
        riqsichiqkuna kaypi?

Will you guide me?
    poo·sah·wahn·kee·*mahn*·choo?

        ¿Pusawankimanchu?

How long is the trail?
    mai·kah·*mah*·tahkh
    poo·reen·*chees*·mahn?

        ¿Maykamataq
        purinchisman?

Is the track well-marked?
    ah·lyeen oo·nahn·chahs·*kah*·choo
    chai nyahn?

        ¿Allin unanchasqachu
        chay ñan?

Which is the shortest route?
    mai·*ken*·tahkh *ahs*·wahn
    pee·see poo·*ree*·nah?

        ¿Mayqintaq aswan
        pisi purina?

Which is the easiest route?
    mai·*ken*·tahkh *mah*·nah
    sah·sah poo·*ree*·nah?

        ¿Mayqintaq mana
        sasa purina?

ALTITUDE SICKNESS

Altitude sickness, *suruchi*, soo·roo·chee, is always a real concern when travelling anywhere in the Andes. Symptoms include:

breathlessness	*mana samayniyuq*
	mah·nah sah·mai·*nee*·yokh
dizziness	*uma muyuy*
	oo·mah *moo*·yui
fatigue	*sayk'uy*
	sai·k'ui
headache	*uma nanay*
	oo·mah *nah*·nai
insomnia	*mana puñuy atipay*
	mah·nah poo·nyui ah·*tee*·pai
mental confusion	*yuyay pantay*
	yoo·yai *pahn*·tai
nausea	*millanayay*
	mee·lyah·*nah*·yai
a pounding heart	*sunqu phatatatay*
	son·ko p·hah·tah·*tah*·tai

If you're on the trail and start to notice symptoms, try to move to a lower altitude immediately. Glucose tablets may also help. Chewing coca leaves, *kuka matu*, koo·kah *mah*·too, is a local remedy that Andeans have used for centuries. If you can't bring yourself to do that, coca leaf tea, *kuka mati*, koo·kah *mah*·tee, might also do the trick. If you're in a city and you experience symptoms, rest and get acclimatised – drink plenty of water – before trying any strenuous activities such as trekking, even for short day trips. Seek medical assistance if the symptoms persist.

How many hours will it take?
   *hai·*k'ah oo·*rahs·*peen   *¿Hayk'a uraspin*
   *chai·*mahn chah·*yahn·*chees?   *chayman chayanchis?*
Is the path open?
   kee·chahs·*kah·*choo   *¿Kichasqachu*
   nyahn *kah·*shahn?   *ñan kashan?*
Is it safe to climb this mountain?
   wee·chah·*nah·*pahkh   *¿Wichanapaq*
   ah·*lyeen·*choo kai *or·*ko?   *allinchu kay urqu?*
How high is the climb?
   mai·kah·*mah·*tahkh   *¿Maykamataq*
   wee·chahn·*chees·*mahn?   *wichanchisman?*
Is there a hut up there?
   *chookh·*lyah kahn·choo   *¿Chuklla kanchu*
   hah·*nahkh·*pee?   *hanaqpi?*

TREKKING

When does it get dark?
   *ee·*mah oo·*rahs·*mee   *¿Ima urasmi*
   too·*tah·*yahn?   *tutayan?*
Where can I hire mountain gear?
   mai·*pee·*tahkh *or·*ko   *¿Maypitaq urqu*
   wee·chah·*nah·*pahkh   *wichanapaq*
   ee·mah·*tah·*pahs   *imatapas*
   ahl·kee·lah·*rui·*mahn?   *alkilarquyman?*
Where can we buy supplies?
   mai·*pee·*tahkh ee·mai·*mah·*nah   *¿Maypitaq imaymana*
   kahkh·koo·*nah·*tah   *kaqkunata*
   rahn·tee·rui·*koo·*mahn?   *rantirquykuman?*
Do you have llamas?
   *kahn·*choo   *¿Kanchu*
   lyah·mai·kee·*koo·*nah?   *llamaykikuna?*

How much do you charge for ...?	hai·*k'ah*·tahn koob·*rahn*·kee ...?	¿*Hayk'atan kubranki* ...?
a day	*sah*·pah p'oon·chai	*sapa p'unchay*
donkeys	ahs·nui·kee·koo·nah· *mahn*·tah	*asnuykikuna- manta*
llamas	lyah·mai·kee·koo·nah· *mahn*·tah	*llamaykikuna- manta*
mules	moo·lai·kee·koo·nah· *mahn*·tah	*mulaykikuna- manta*
a tent	kahr·pai·kee·*mahn*·tah	*karpaykimanta*

ON THE PATH ÑANPI

Could you tell me the way to ...?
mai·*teen*·tahn ....mahn
reen·chees?

¿*Maynintan* ...-*man rinchis?*

Does this path go to ...?
....mahn *reen*·choo kai nyahn?

¿...-*man rinchu kay ñan?*

Where have you come from?
mai·mahn·*tah*·tahkh
hah·moo·*rahn*·kee?

¿*Maymantataq hamurqanki?*

How long did it take you?
hai·k'ah p'oon·chai·*pee*·tahkh
chah·yah·rah·*moon*·kee?

¿*Hayk'a p'unchaypitaq chayarqamunki?*

Where's the nearest village?
mai·*pee*·tahkh *kah*·shahn
lyoo·*mahn*·tah ahs·wahn sees·pah
lyahkh·*tah*·kah?

¿*Maypitaq kashan lliwmanta aswan sispa llaqtaqa?*

Where can we spend the night?
mai·*pee*·tahkh
poo·nyoo·pah·koo·yoo·kui·mahn?

¿*Maypitaq puñupakuyukuyman?*

Can I leave some things here
for a while?
pahkh·tah rah·too·kah·*mah*·lyah
k'e·pee·koo·*nah*·tah
sah·ke·yoo·kui·*kee*·mahn *kai*·pee?

¿*Paqta ratukamalla q'ipikunata saqiyukuykiman kaypi?*

May I cross your property?
  chahk·*rai*·kekh keen·rai·*lyahm*·tah   ¿*Chakraykiq*
  pah·sai·*mahn*·choo?   *kinrayllanta pasaymanchu?*
Can we go through here?
  kai·*neen*·tah   ¿*Kayninta*
  poo·ree·koo·*mahn*·choo?   *puriykumanchu?*
Is this water OK to drink?
  ah·*lyeen*·choo   ¿*Allinchu*
  ook·yah·*nah*·pahkh kai *oo*·noo?   *ukyanapaq kay unu?*
I'm lost.
  cheen·*kahs*·kahn poo·ree·*shah*·nee   *Chinkasqan purishani.*

altitude	*sah*·yai	*sayay*
altitude sickness	soo·*roo*·chee	*suruchi*
backpack	*k'e*·pee	*q'ipi*
candle	*bee*·lah	*bila*
to climb	wee·chai/*se*·kai	*wichay/siqay*
downhill	*oo*·rai	*uray*
first-aid kit	*hahm*·pee choo·*rah*·nah	*hampi churana*
gloves	*wahm*·tees	*wantis*
guide	*poo*·sahkh	*pusaq*
guided trek	poo·*sahkh*·wahn *poo*·ree	*pusaqwan puriy*
hike/to hike	*poo*·ree	*puriy*
hunting	*chah*·koo	*chaku*
hut	ch'*ookh*·lyah	*ch'uklla*
lookout	k-hah·*wah*·nah	*qhawana*
map	*mah*·pah	*mapa*
mountain climbing	*or*·ko wee·chai	*urqu wichay*
pick (tool)	*pee*·koo	*piku*
provisions (food)	*ko*·kow	*quqaw*
provisions (things)	kahkh·*koo*·nah	*kaqkuna*
rock climbing	*kah*·kah wee·chai	*qaqa wichay*
rope	*wahs*·k-hah	*waskha*
signpost	oo·*nahn*·chah	*unancha*
steep	*sah*·yahkh	*sayaq*
trek/to trek	*kah*·roo *poo*·ree	*karu puriy*
uphill	wee·chai/*hah*·nai	*wichay/hanay*
to walk	*poo*·ree	*puriy*

TREKKING

TREKKING

CAMPING   KARPA RUWAY

Designated camp sites exist only in tourist places like Machu Picchu or Sacsayhuamán. As long as you have permission from the locals, you can pitch your tent almost anywhere.

Is there a camp site nearby?
  kahn·choo kai·pee pahm·pah   *¿Kanchu kaypi pampa*
  kahr·pah·pahkh?   *karpapaq?*
Can we camp here?
  kahr·pah·tah   *¿Karpata*
  roo·wai·koo·mahn·choo   *ruwaykumanchu*
  kai·pee?   *kaypi?*
Who owns this land?
  pekh·tahkh kai chahkh·rah?   *¿Piqtaq kay chakra?*
Can I talk to him/her?
  ree·mai·mahn·choo pai·wahn?   *¿Rimaymanchu paywan?*
Where can I hire a tent?
  mai·pee·tahkh kahr·pah·tah   *¿Maypitaq karpata*
  ahl·kee·lah·rui·mahn?   *alkilarquyman?*
Are there shower facilities?
  kahn·choo bah·nyoo   *¿Kanchu bañu*
  ahr·mah·koo·nah·pahkh?   *armakunapaq?*

blanket	*choo*·see/*kah*·tah/	*chusi/qatal*
	mahn·tah	*manta*
camping	kahm·pah·*meen*·too	*kampamintu*
camp site	kahr·*pah*·pahkh	*karpapaq*
	pahm·pah	*pampa*
firewood	*lyahm*·t'ah	*llant'a*
hammer	tah·*kah*·nah	*takana*
hammock	ah·*mah*·kah	*amaka*
knife	koo·*chee*·lyoo/	*kuchillu/*
	koo·*choo*·nah	*kuchuna*
matches	p-hoos·*poo*·roo	*phuspuru*
mattress (bedding)	poo·*nyoo*·nah	*puñuna*
rope	*wahs*·k·hah	*waskha*
sleeping bag	poo·*nyoo*·nah	*puñuna*
tent (pegs)	*kahr*·pah	*karpa*
	(tah·kahr·poo·*koo*·nah)	*(takarpukuna)*
torch (flashlight)	k'ahn·*chah*·nah/	*k'anchana/*
	leen·*teer*·nah	*lintirna*
water	oo·noo/*yah*·koo	*unu/yaku*
water bottle	woo·*tee*·lyah	*wutilla*
	oo·noo/*yah*·koo	*unu/yaku*

TREKKING

WEATHER   PACHA/TIMPU

What's the weather like?
    ee·*mai*·nahn *pah*·chah/   ¿*Imaynan pacha/*
    teem·poo *kah*·shahn?   *timpu kashan?*
What's the forecast for tomorrow?
    ee·*mai*·nahn *pah*·chah/   ¿*Imaynan pacha/*
    teem·poo *kahn*·kah   *timpu kanqa*
    pah·*kah*·reen?   *paqarin?*

Today it's ...	...shahn *koo*·nahn	...-shan kunan
	p'oon·chai	*p'unchay.*
cold/chilly	*chee*·ree	*chiri*
hot/sunny	*roo*·p·hah	*rupha*
windy	*seen*·chee *wai*·rah	*sinchi wayra*

It's raining heavily.
    nee·*shoo*·tahn pah·*rah*·shahn   *Nishutan parashan.*
It's raining lightly.
    pee·see·*lyah*·tahn pah·*rah*·shahn   *Pisillatan parashan.*
It's flooding.
    lyok·lyah·*shahn*·mee   *Lluqllashanmi.*

cloud	*p-hoo*·yoo	*phuyu*
dew	*ch-hoo*·lyah	*chhulla*
drizzle	*ee*·p-hoo	*iphu*
dry season	*ch'ah*·kee *mee*·tah	*ch'aki mita*
fog/mist	*pah*·chah p-hoo·yoo	*pacha phuyu*
frost	*kah*·sah/*k-hoo*·pah	*qasa/qhupa*
glacier	*ree*·t'ee	*rit'i*
hail	*cheek*·chee	*chikchi*
hot	*roo*·p-hoo	*rupha*
ice	ch-hoo·*lyoon*·koo	*chhullunku*
lightning	ee·*lyah*·pah/	*illapa/*
	lyeef·*lyee*	*lliphlli*
rain	*pah*·rah	*para*
rainy season	*pah*·rai *mee*·tah	*paray mita*
shade	*lyahn*·t-hoo	*llanthu*
snow	*ree*·t'ee	*rit'i*
storm	*lyokh*·lyah *pah*·rah	*lluqlla para*
sun	*een*·tee	*inti*
sunny	*roo*·p-hah	*rupha*
thunder	*k-hahkh*·yah	*qhaqya*
warm	toom·pah·*lyah*·tah	*tumpallata*
	roo·p-hah	*rupha*
wind	*wai*·rah	*wayra*
windy	*seen*·chee *wai*·rah	*sinchi wayra*

GEOGRAPHICAL TERMS

PACHA SUTIKUNA

cave	*mah*·ch'ai	*mach'ay*
cliff	*kah*·kah	*qaqa*
earthquake	*pah*·chah *koo*·yui	*pacha kuyu*
forest	*mahly*·kee *mahly*·kee	*mallki mallki*
gap	*k'eekh*·lyoo	*k'ikllu*
high plateau	*poo*·nah/*sahly*·kah	*puna/sallqa*
hill	*or*·ko·chah/*mo*·ko	*urqucha/muqu*
hot spring	*k'o*·nee *pook*·yoo	*q'uñi pukyu*
hot valley	*yoon*·kah	*yunka*
lake	*ko*·chah	*qucha*
mountain	*or*·ko	*urqu*
mountain path	*or*·ko·pee nyahn	*urqupi ñan*
pass (narrow)	*k'ah*·sah	*q'asa*
peak	*or*·kohk *poon*·tahn	*urquq puntan*
ravine	*wai*·k'o	*wayq'u*
river	*mah*·yoo	*mayu*
sea	ko·chah·*mah*·mah	*quchamama*
snow line	*ree*·t'ee *se*·ke	*rit'i siqi*
stone/rock	*roo*·meel/*wahn*·k'ah	*rumi/wank'a*
volcano	*nee*·nah p·*hokh*·chekh *or*·ko	*nina phuqchiq urqu*
waterfall	p·*hahkh*·chah/p·*how*·chee	*phaqcha/phawchi*

TREKKING

TREKKING

FAUNA   IMAYMANA ANIMALKUNA

What animal is that?
  ee·mah ah·nee·*mahl*·tahkh chai?   ¿Ima animaltaq chay?

Domestic Creatures   Uywakuna

alpaca	ahl·*pah*·kah	*alpaka*
cat	mee·see/*mee*·chee	*misi/michi*
dog	*ahl*·ko/*aly*·ko	*alqu/allqu*
donkey	*ahs*·noo	*asnu*
goat	*kow*·rah	*kawra*
horse	kah·*wah*·lyoo	*kawallu*
guanaco	wah·*nah*·koo	*wanaku*
(like a llama)		
llama	*lyah*·mah	*llama*
mule	*moo*·lah	*mula*
ox	*too*·roo	*turu*
pig	k-*hoo*·chee	*khuchi*
sheep	*ook*·yah/oo·*wee*·hah	*ukya/uwiha*

Birds   Pisqukuna

Andean flamingo	pah·ree·*wah*·nah	*pariwana*
Andean songbird	*poo*·kui *poo*·kui	*pukuy pukuy*
condor	*koon*·toor	*kuntur*
wild duck	*choo*·lyoo *mah*·yoo	*chullu mayu*
eagle	*ahn*·kah	*anka*
falcon/hawk	*wah*·mahn	*waman*
hummingbird	(*ko*·ree) *k'en*·tee	*(quri) q'inti*
owl	*too*·koo/*hoo*·koo	*tuku/huku*
partridge	*yoo*·t-hoo/*lyoo*·t-hoo	*yuthu/lluthu*
rooster	*k'ahn*·kah	*k'anka*
seagull	*kely*·wah/*kyoo*·lyah/	*qillwa/qiwlla/*
	kely·*wai*·too	*qillwaytu*
sparrowhawk	*ahn*·kah/*wah*·mahn	*anka/waman*
turtledove	*kooly*·koo	*kullku*
vulture	soo·we·*k'ah*·rah	*suwiq'ara*
woodpecker	hah·*k'ahkh*·lyoo	*hak'akllu*

Wildlife | Salqa Animalkuna

armadillo	keer·*keen*·choo	*kirkinchu*
bear	oo·*koo*·koo	*ukuku*
deer	tah·*roo*·kah	*taruka*
fish	*chahly*·wah	*challwa*
fox	*ah*·tokh	*atuq*
frog	hahm·*p'ah*·too	*hamp'atu*
game (animals)	chah·koo·*nah*·pahkh	*chakunapaq*
	ah·nee·mahl·*koo*·nah	*animalkuna*
leech	*yah*·wahr *ch'on*·kahkh	*yawar ch'unqaq*
lizard	soo·koo·*lyoo*·koo/	*sukulluku/*
	kah·*rai*·wah	*qaraywa*
monkey	koo·*see*·lyoo	*kusillu*
mountain lion	*poo*·mah	*puma*
snake	mah·*ch'ahkh*·wai/	*mach'aqway/*
	ah·*mah*·roo	*amaru*
spider	ah·*rah*·nyah;	*araña;*
	koo·see·*koo*·see	*kusi-kusi*
trout	*troo*·chah	*trucha*
turtle	chah·*rah*·pah	*charapa*
vicuña	wee·*k'oo*·nyah	*wik'uña*
(like a llama)		
viscacha (rodent)	wees·*k'ah*·chah	*wisk'acha*
wildcat	os·k·ho·lyoo	*usqhullu*
wild pig	see·*wai*·roo	*siwayru*

Insects | Kuru

bee	lah·*chee*·wah	*lachiwa*
butterfly	peely·*peen*·too	*pillpintu*
cockroach	koo·kah·*rah*·chah	*kukaracha*
dung beetle	*ah*·kah *tahn*·kah	*aka tanqa*
flea	*pee*·kee	*piki*
fly	*ch'oos*·pee	*ch'uspi*
louse/lice	oo·sah/oo·sah·*koo*·nah	*usa/usakuna*
mosquito	k·he·te (*ch'oos*·pee)	*qhiti (ch'uspi)*

TREKKING

TREKKING

THE LEGEND OF THE INCAS

At the beginning of time, near Lake Titicaca high in the Peruvian Andes, in a place known as Paqariqtampu, *pah·kah·rekh·tahm·poo*, there appeared four brothers and four sisters, who were all children of the Sun, the highest of deities. The Sun charged these brothers and sisters with teaching humankind the principles of civilization, truth and justice. For this purpose, he gave them a golden staff, with which they were to seek out the ideal site to found an empire. They would know this site when the staff was swallowed up completely by the earth, upon striking the ground.

The brothers and sisters began their search for an empire by first organising the people living around Paqariqtampu into *ayllus*, *ai·lyoos*, or communities. They taught the people to cultivate the land, weave fibres and build houses; about laws, wars and the religion of the Sun. After this, everyone departed in search of their promised land, and *Manqu Khapaq*, *mahn·ko k·hah·pahkh*, and *Mama Uqllu*, *mah·mah okh·lyo*, the principal figures of the divine family, struck the ground every day with the magic staff. Finally, they arrived near a hill called Wanakawri, *wah·nah·kow·ree*, where, with the first strike, the golden staff disappeared. *Manqu Khapaq* and *Mama Uqllu* decided to establish the city of Qusqu, *kos·ko*, or 'Cuzco', which became the centre of their empire, Tawantinsuyu, *tah·wahn·teen·soo·yoo*, meaning 'four parts or regions (of the empire)'.

FLORA & AGRICULTURE

MALLKI MALLKIPAS CHAKRA RURUPAS

Trees, Plants & Flowers

Sach'akunapas Yurakunapas

What ... is that?	ee·mah ... chai?	¿Ima ... chay?
tree	sah·ch'ah·tahkh	sach'ataq
plant	yoo·rah·tahkh	yurataq
flower	t'ee·kah·tahkh	t'ikataq
agave (aloe)	pahkh·pah	paqpa
broom (bush)	t'ahn·kahr	t'anqar
cactus	k'ahkh·lyah/	k'aklla/
	ah·nyah·pahn·koo	añapanku
cactus fruit	too·nahs	tunas
coca	koo·kah	kuka
eucalyptus	yoo·kah·leekh·too	yukaliptu
medlar	wees·wee·roo	wiswiru
mountain grass	ee·ch·hoo	ichhu
nettle	kee·sah/k'oo·rah	kisa/k'ura
pine	pee·noo	pinu
quingual	keen·wahl	kinwal
(Andean tree)		
scrub	ch'ah·p-hrah	ch'aphra
thorn/spine	kees·kah	kiska
totora reed	t'oo·too·rah	t'utura
white poplar	kees·wahr	kiswar
wild cherry tree	kah·poo·lee	kapuli

Herbs & Crops

Qurakunapis, Rurukunapis

beans	ahl·weer·hahs	alwirhas
cabbage	koo·lees	kulis
coriander (cilantro)	koo·lahn·troo	kulantru
corn	sah·rah	sara
fava beans	hah·wahs	hawas
flower	t'ee·kah/wai·tah	t'ika/wayta

TREKKING

TREKKING

garlic	*ah*·hoos	*ahus*
huacatay (aromatic herb)	wah·*kah*·tai	*wakatay*
kiwicha (grain)	kee·*wee*·chah	*kiwicha*
leaf	*rah*·p-heel/*rah*·p'ah	*raphi/rap'a*
lemon tree	*lee*·moon *sah*·ch'ah	*limun sach'a*
lupine	*tahr*·wee	*tarwi*
mashua (local tuber)	*ah*·nyoo/*mahs*·wah	*añu/maswa*
oca (tuber)	o·kah	*uqa*
onion	see·*wee*·lyah	*siwilla*
orange tree	lah·*rahm*·hah *sah*·ch'ah	*laranha sach'a*
orchard	*moo*·yah	*muya*
papaya (highland)	pah·*pah*·yah	*papaya*
parsley	pee·*ree*·heel	*pirihil*
peas	ahl·*weer*·hahs	*alwirhas*
potatoes	*pah*·pah	*papa*
quinoa	*kyoo*·nah/*kyoo*·nyah	*kiwna/kiwña*
tree	*mahly*·kee	*mallki*
wheat	*tree*·yoo	*triyu*
yacón (tuber)	*lyah*·kom/*yah*·koo	*llaqum/yaku*

SHOPPING

Use Quechua for building a rapport with market vendors.

LOOKING FOR ...   ... MASKHAY

Where's a/the nearest ...?	mai·*pee*·tahkh ... kahn?	¿Maypitaq ... kan?
bank	*kol*·ke *wah*·see	qulqi wasi
market	k·*hah*·too	qhatu
music shop	moo·*see*·kah *teen*·dah	musika tinda
pharmacy	hahm·*pee*·yokh *wah*·see	hampiyuq wasi
shoe shop	sah·*pah*·too *teen*·dah	sapatu tinda
shop	*teen*·dah	tinda

Where can I buy (a) ...?	mai·*pee*·tahkh ... rahn·tee·*rui*·mahn?	¿Maypitaq ... rantirquyman?
book	lyoo·roo·koo·*nah*·tah	liwrukunata
clothes	p'ah·chah·koo·*nah*·tah	p'achakunata
handicrafts	ahr·tee·sah·nee·yah·koo·*nah*·tah	artisaniyakunata
souvenirs	*too*·kui *reek*·ch'ahkh ee·mai·mah·nah·koo·*nah*·tah	tukuy rikch'aq imaymanakunata

Where can I get a haircut?
    mai·*pee*·tahkh chook·*chai*·tah roo·too·chee·koo·*rui*·mahn?

¿Maypitaq chukchayta rutuchikurquyman?

MAKING A PURCHASE   RANTIY

I'd like to buy ...
    ...·tah rahn·*tee*·tahn moo·*nai*·mahn

...-ta rantiytan munayman.

I'm just looking.
    k·hah·*wai*·lyahn k·hah·wah·*shah*·nee

Qhawayllan qhawashani.

Can you write down the price?
    chah·*neen*·tah kel·kahn·kee·*mahn*·choo?

¿Chaninta qilqankimanchu?

Can I look at it?
  k·hah·wai·kui·*mahn*·choo?   *¿Qhawaykuymanchu?*

Do you have any others?
  hokh·*koo*·nah   *¿Huqkuna*
  kah·poo·soon·*kee*·choo?   *kapusunkichu?*

I don't like it.
  mah·nahn *kai*·tah   *Manan kayta*
  moo·nah·*nee*·choo   *munanichu.*

OK, I'll buy it.
  ah·*lyeen*,·mee *chai*·tah   *Allinmi, chayta*
  ah·pah·*koo*·sahkh/   *apakusaq/rantisaq.*
  rahn·*tee*·sahkh

How much is it all together?
  hai·k'ahn lyoo·*neen*·koo?   *¿Hayk'an lliwninku?*

Could I have a receipt please?
  ree·see·*woo*·tah   *¿Risiwuta*
  ko·wahn·kee·*mahn*·choo?   *quwankimanchu?*

I want to exchange this.
  kai·tah kahm·bee·*yai*·tah   *Kayta kambiyayta*
  moo·*nah*·nee   *munani.*

It's faulty.
  mah·nahn kai ah·*lyeen*·choo   *Manan kay allinchu.*

I'd like my money back.
  kol·*kee*·tah koo·tee·chee·*poo*·wai   *Qulqiyta kutichipuway.*

THEY MAY SAY ...

yow *(tai*·tah *reen*·goo; *mah*·mah *reen*·gah)!
  Listen (Sir/Madam)!

ee·mah·lyah·*tah*·pahs rahn·*tee*·wai, tai·*tai*/mah·*mai*
  Please buy something from me, Sir/Madam.

hai·*k'ah*·tahn moo·*nahn*·kee?
  How much/many do you want?

chah·*neen*·tah pee·see·yah·*chee*·sahkh *ree*·kee
  I'll lower the price for you.

BARGAINING CHANINTA PISIYACHIY

Bargaining is a widespread practice in Latin America, especially in Peru. You can bargain for just about anything, except perhaps your bill at a fine restaurant or the cost of something at a department store. You'll definitely be expected to bargain with street or market sellers.

How much is this?
hai·*k'ah*·tahkh chai? *¿Hayk'ataq chay?*

Really?
che·*kahkh*·choo? *¿Chiqaqchu?*

The price is too high.
seen·chee chah·nee·*yokh*·mee chai *Sinchi chaniyuqmi chay.*

It's too much for me.
mah·nahn kol·kay *Manan qulqiy*
ai·pah·*wahn*·choo *aypawanchu.*

Can you lower the price?
chah·*neen*·tah *¿Chaninta*
pee·see·yah·cheen·kee·*mahm*·choo/ *pisiyachinkimanchu/*
oo·rai·kah·cheen·kee·*mahm*·choo? *uraykachinkimanchu?*

Do you have something cheaper?
mah·nah ahn·chah chah·*nee*·yokh *¿Mana ancha chaniyuq*
ee·mah·*lyai*·kee·pahs *imallaykipas*
kah·poo·soon·*kee*·choo? *kapusunkichu?*

Is that your final price?
chai·choo *chah*·neen *ree*·kee? *¿Chaychu chanin riki?*

I'll give you ...
...tah koy·koo·*sai*·kee *...-ta quykusayki.*

SHOPPING

SOUVENIRS IMAYMANAKUNA RANTINAPAQ

baskets	ai·sah·nah·*koo*·nah/	*aysanakuna/*
	p'ookh·too·*koo*·nah/	*p'uktukuna/*
	kah·nahs·tah·*koo*·nah	*kanastakuna*
handicrafts	ahr·tee·sah·nee·yah·*koo*·nah	*artisaniyakuna*
jewellery	ee·lyah/oo·mee·nyah	*illa/umiña*

SHOPPING

masks	oo·yah·tee·*koo*·nah	*uyatikuna*
musical	moo·*see*·kah	*musika*
instruments	wah·kah·chee·nah·*koo*·nah	*waqachinakuna*
pottery	*rahkh*·chee/*k'ahkh*·rah	*raqchi/k'akra*
shell souvenirs	ch'oo·roo·*mahn*·tah	*ch'urumanta*
	roo·*wahs*·kah	*ruwasqa*
	ee·mah·mai·nah·*koo*·nah	*imamaynakuna*
tapestries	t'e·ke·*koo*·nah	*t'iqikuna*
wood carvings	k'oo·lyoo·*mahn*·tah	*k'ullumanta*
	roo·*wahs*·kah	*ruwasqa*
	reekh·ch'ay	*rikch'ay*
woven textiles	ah·wai·*koo*·nah	*awaykuna*

CLOTHING   P'ACHA

bag	wah·*yah*·kah	*wayaqa*
belt (Andean)	*choom*·pee	*chumpi*
blanket	*kah*·tah/*choo*·see/	*qata/chusi/*
boots	*boo*·tahs	*butas*
cap (Andean)	ch'oo·lyoo	*ch'ullu*
dress	p'ah·chah	*p'acha*
handbag	ch'oos·pah	*ch'uspa*
hat	soom·*ree*·roo	*sumriru*
jacket	*sah*·koo	*saku*
jeans	pahn·*tah*·loon	*pantalun*
jumper (sweater)	*choom*·pah	*chumpa*
poncho	*poon*·choo	*punchu*
purse	ch'oos·pah	*ch'uspa*
scarf	chah·*lee*·nah	*chalina*
shawl	lyeekh·lyah	*lliklla*
shirt	kah·*mee*·sah	*kamisa*
shoes	sah·pah·too·*koo*·nah	*sapatukuna*
skirt	poo·*lyee*·rah	*pullira*
socks	*mee*·dyahs	*midyas*
T-shirt	*oon*·k·hoo/	*unkhu/*
	kah·mee·*see*·tah	*kamisita*

Can I try it on?
    choo·rah·kui·koo·*mahn*·choo   *¿Churakuykumanchu*
    chai·tah?   *chayta?*
It doesn't fit.
    mah·nahn sah·yai·*nee*·choo   *Manan sayayniychu.*

It's too ...   *kai*·kah ...·*mee*/·n   *Kayqa ...-mi/-n.*
  big   *hah*·toon   *hatun*
  large   *seen*·chee *hah*·toon   *sinchi hatun*
  long   *wahs*·k'ah   *wask'a*
  small   *hoo*·chui   *huchuy*
  short   *teen*·koo/*tahkh*·sah   *tinku/taksa*
  tight   *k'ees*·kee   *k'iski*

MATERIALS   IMATAPAS RUWANAPAQ

bamboo	to·*ko*·ro/*so*·kos	*tuquru/suqus*
bone	*too*·lyoo	*tullu*
ceramic	*rahkh*·chee/*k'ahkh*·rah	*raqch'i/k'akra*
clay	*lyahn*·k'ee/*lyeen*·k'ee	*llank'i/llink'i*
cotton	*oot*·k·hoo	*utkhu*
handmade	mah·*kee*·wahn	*makiwan*
	roo·*wahs*·kah	*ruwasqa*
fabric	*lyee*·kah/*ah*·wah	*llika/awa*
glass	*kes*·pee	*qispi*
gold	*ko*·ree	*quri*
horn	*wahkh*·rah	*waqra*
leather	*kah*·rah	*qara*
metal	*ahn*·tah/*tee*·tee	*anta/titi*
plastic	plahs·*tee*·koo	*plastiku*
reed	*so*·kos/*k'oor*·koor	*suqus/k'urkur*
silver	*kol*·ke	*qulqi*
stainless steel	ah·*see*·roo	*asiru*
stone	*roo*·mee	*rumi*
straw	*ee*·ch·hoo	*ichhu*
thread	*k'ai*·too	*q'aytu*
wood	*k'oo*·lyoo	*k'ullu*
wool	*meely*·mah/*meely*·wah	*millma/millwa*

SHOPPING

COLOURS

black	*yah*·nah
blue	*ahn*·kahs/*ah*·sool
brown	*ch'oom*·pee
colour	*lyeem*·p'ee/*koo*·loor/ *tooly*·pee
green	*k'o*·mer
grey	*o*·ke/*ch'ekh*·chee/*tee*·tee
orange	*wee·lah*·pee
pink	*pahn*·tee; *lyahn*·k·hah *poo*·kah
purple	*koo*·lyee/*moo·rah*·roo
red	*poo*·kah
white	*yoo*·rahkh
yellow	*k'e*·lyoo

LLIMP'IKUNA

yana
anqas/asul
ch'umpi
llimp'i/kulur/
tullpi
q'umir
uqi/ch'iqchi/titi
wilapi
panti;
llanqha puka
kulli/muraru
puka
yuraq
q'illu

WOOLLY LOGIC

In the Andes, several wool-producing animals have been domesticated and are clipped for their wool. These include alpacas *(alpaka,* **ahl·pah·kah),** guanacos *(wanaku,* **wah·nah·koo)** sheep *(ukya/uwiha,* **ook·yah/oo·wee·hah)** and llamas *(llama, lyah·mah).* The alpaca-like vicuña *(wik'uña,* **wee·k'oo·nyah),** an undomesticated species, was once hunted for its wool, but it's now considered endangered. No matter what its source, the word for wool in Quechua is *millma, meely·mah,* or its variant, *millwa, meely·wah.*

Wool can be used to make a range of clothing and accessories which traditionally exhibit a variety of regional motifs *(pallay, pah·lyai).* Common designs include coca and potato flowers, llamas, alpacas and vicuñas, mountains, cacti, the Inca figure, masks, patterns of multi-coloured lines, birds, and silhouettes of towns and people working or socialising.

TOILETRIES   SUMAQYACHIQKUNA

comb	*nyahkh·ch'ah*	*ñaqch'a*
razor	*soon·k·hah roo·too·nah/*	*sunkha rutuna/*
	k'ee·soo·nah	*k'isuna*
shampoo	*chahm·poo*	*champu*
soap	*hah·woon*	*hawun*
tissues	*sen·kah pee·chah·nah*	*sinqa pichana*
toothbrush	*kee·roo k·he·too·nah*	*kiru qhituna*

FOR THE BABY   WAWACHAPAQ

baby powder	**wah·*wah*·pahkh *tahl*·koo**	*wawapaq talku*
bib	**bah·*bee*·roo**	*babiru*
bottle	**bee·*bee*·roon**	*bibirun*
nappies/diapers	**ah·kah·*wah*·rah/**	*akawara/*
	wahl·*t'ah*·nah	*walt'ana*
dummy/pacifier	**nyoo·*nyoo*·nah**	*ñuñuna*
teat	**nyoo·nyoo**	*ñuñu*

SMOKING   PITAY

Smoking is much more common among men than women; traditionally, it's unacceptable for women to smoke. As times have changed, some women have taken it up, especially the *hampiq, hahm·pekh*, or folk healers. You should ask if it's OK to light up when in close proximity to others.

Do you sell cigarettes here?
    see·yah·roo·koo·*nah*·tah   *¿Siyarukunata*
    been·deen·*kee*·choo?   *bindinkichu?*

Do you smoke?
    pee·tahn·*kee*·choo kahn?   *¿Pitankichu qan?*

Do you have a light?
    foos·poo·*rui*·kee *kahn*·choo?   *¿Phuspuruyki kanchu?*

Do you mind if I smoke?
    pee·tai·*mahn*·choo kai·pee?   *¿Pitaymanchu kaypi?*

Please don't smoke.
    ah·*lyee*·choo *ah*·mah pee·*tai*·choo   *Allichu ama pitaychu.*

SHOPPING

cigarettes	see·*yah*·roo	*siyaru*
cigars	*hah*·toon ch'oom·pee	*hatun ch'umpi*
	see·*yah*·roo	*siyaru*
lighter	*nee*·nah rah·tah·*chee*·nah;	*nina ratachina;*
	k'ahn·chah·*chee*·nah	*k'anchachina*
matches	foos·*poo*·roo	*phuspuru*
tobacco	tah·*wah*·koo	*tawaku*

SIZES & COMPARISONS   SAYAYKUNAPAS TINKUCHIKUYKUNAPAS

a little bit	pee·see·*lyah*·tah/	*pisillata/*
	toom·pah·*lyah*·tah	*tumpallata*
also	...·pees/·pahs	*...-pis/-pas*
big	*hah*·toon	*hatun*
enough	chai·*lyah*·nyah	*chayllaña*
heavy	*lyah*·sahkh	*llasaq*
light	ch·*hah*·lyah	*chhalla*
little (amount)	pee·see/*toom*·pah	*pisi/tumpa*
many	*ahs*·k·hah/ch·*hee*·kah	*askha/chhika*
more	*ahs*·wahn	*aswan*
small	*hoo*·chui	*huchuy*
too much/ many	*ahs*·k·hah *ahs*·k·hah; ch·*hee*·kah ch·*hee*·kah	*askha askha; chhika chhika*

MIKHUNA   FOOD

A great variety of dishes and cuisine is available throughout the
Andes. In most restaurants, staff will speak Spanish, so Quechua
will be more useful for visits to local markets, fairs, festivals and
small restaurants.

THROUGH THE DAY   P'UNCHAYNINTIN

Since rural Andeans rise with the sun, breakfast may be as early
as five or six o'clock in the morning. Lunch, the biggest meal of
the day, is at midday, while dinner is around six in the evening.
Bedtime is generally at nightfall. This routine varies for festivals
and holidays, when everyone has a chance to party.

breakfast	*mah·*tee; *oo·*noo *k'o·*nyee	*mati; unu q'uñi*
lunch	ahl·*moo·*sai/*mee·*k-hui	*almusay/mikhuy*
dinner	*too·*tah *mee·*k-hui; *see·*nah	*tuta mikhuy; sina*

SPECIAL   QHALI KAYPAQ
DIETS   MIKHUYKUNA

Meat is an integral part of the Andean diet, even though it may
be served in small quantities. You won't find vegetarian meals in
small rural restaurants or when staying at someone's home.

Does this dish have meat in it?
   ai·chah·*yokh·*choo kai
   mee·*k-hoo·*nah?
              ¿Aychayuqchu kay
              mikhuna?
Can I get this without meat?
   *mah·*nah ai·chah·*yohkh·*tah
   kah·rai·koo·wahn·kee·*mahn·*choo
   *kai·*tah?
              ¿Mana aychayuqta
              qaraykuwankimanchu
              kayta?

I don't eat meat.
*mah·*nahn ai·*chah*·tah
mee·k·hoo·*nee*·choo

*Manan aychata
mikhunichu.*

I don't eat chicken or fish.
*mah·*nahn *wahly·*pah ai·*chah*·tah,
*chahly·*wah ai·*chah*·tah
mee·k·hoo·*nee*·choo

*Manan wallpa aychata,
challwa aychata
mikhunichu.*

I can't eat dairy products.
*mah·*nah lee·chee·*mahn·*tah
roo·*wahs*·kah
mee·k·hui·koo·*nah·*tah
mee·*k·hui*·tah ah·tee·*nee*·choo

*Manan lichimanta
ruwasqa
mikhuykunata
mikhuyta atinichu.*

Does it contain egg?
roon·too·*yohkh*·choo kai·kah?

¿Runtuyuqchu kayqa?

I'm allergic to (peanuts).
*mah·*nahn (mah·*nee*)·tah
mee·k·hoo·*nee*·choo.
ah·leer·*hee*·koon *kah*·nee

*Manan (mani)-ta
mikhunichu.
Alirhikun kani.*

EATING OUT

MIKHUNA WASIPIPAS KARPAPIPAS MIKHUY

Eating out in rural areas means eating communally outdoors during festivals, fairs or Sunday market days. Local dishes are easily found in *chicherías*, or *chicha* bars – aqha wasikuna, *ah·*khah wah·see·*koo·*nah – and *picanterías*, inexpensive restaurants specialising in spicy dishes. For particularly spicy food, try dishes labelled *arequipeña*, 'Arequipa style', or *a la criolla*, 'Creole style'.

Is there anything to eat?
*kahn·*choo ee·mah·*lyah*·pahs
mee·k·hoo·*nah·*pahkh?

*¿Kanchu imallapas
mikhunapaq?*

Yes, there is.
ah·*ree, kahn·*mee

Arí, kanmi.

No, there isn't.
*mah·*nahn *kahn·*choo

Manan kanchu.

Could you recommend something?
   ee·mah·*tah*·tahkh
   mee·k·hoo·*rui*·mahn?
                        ¿Imatataq
                        mikhurquyman?

Is there any salad?
   een·sah·*lah*·dah *kahn*·choo?
                        ¿Insalada kanchu?

I'll have what they're having.
   pai·*koo*·nah
   mee·k·hoo·shahn·*koo*·tah
   no·*kah*·pahs moo·*nah*·nee
                        Paykuna
                        mikhushankuta
                        nuqapas munani.

What's in that dish?
   ee·mah·*yokh*·mee chai
   mee·k·hoo·nah?
                        ¿Imayuqmi chay
                        mikhuna?

COMPLIMENTS TO THE CHEF

I love this dish.
   kai mee·k·hoo·*nah*·tah
   ahn·*chah*·tah moo·*nah*·nee
                    Kay mikhunata
                    anchata munani.

I'm satisfied/full.
   sahkh·*sahs*·kah *kah*·nee
                    Saksasqa kani.

We love the local cuisine.
   kai lyahkh·*tah*·pee
   mee·k·hoo·*nah*·tah
   seen·*chee*·tah moo·*nai*·koo
                    Kay llaqtapi
                    mikhunata
                    sinchita munayku.

That was delicious!
   soo·mahkh mee·k·hoo·nah!
                    ¡Sumaq mikhuna!

You're an excellent cook.
   koo·sah wai·*k'okh*·mee
   kahn·kee
                    Kusa wayk'uqmi
                    kanki.

FOOD

I want cold/hot water please.
    ah·*lyee*·choo *chee*·reel/k'o·nyee   *Allichu chiri/q'uñi*
    oo·*noo*·tah moo·*nah*·nee   *unuta munani.*
May I have some more please?
    ah·*lyee*·choo   *Allichu*
    yah·pah·yoo·wahn·*kee*·mahn   *yapayuwankiman.*

Please give me a/an/the ...	ah·*lyee*·choo ....tah ko·wai	*Allichu ...-ta quway.*
ashtray	*oosh*·pah choo·*rah*·nah	*ushpa churana*
bill	*kween*·tah	*kwinta*
cup	*sui*·k'oo/ chui·*k'oo*·chah/ *poo*·koo	*suyk'u/ chuyk'ucha/ puku*
fork	tee·*nee*·roor	*tinirur*
knife	koo·*chee*·lyoo	*kuchillu*
plate	*p'oo*·koo/p'oo·*koo*·chah	*p'uku/p'ukucha*
pot	*mahn*·kah	*manka*
spoon	koo·*chah*·rah	*kuchara*
water	oo·noo/*yah*·koo	*unu/yaku*

to boil	t'eem·*poo*·chee	*t'impuchiy*
boiled	t'eem·*poos*·kah	*t'impusqa*
bread (stale)	*choo*·choo t'*ahn*·tah	*chuchu t'anta*
clean (things)	leem·*pee*·yoo/*lui*·loo	*limpiyu/luylu*
clean (water)	ch'oo·yah	*ch'uya*
cold	*chee*·ree	*chiri*
to cook	*wai*·k'ui	*wayk'uy*
cooked	chah·*yahs*·kah	*chayasqa*

dirty	k-he·lyee/k-hahr·kah	qhilli/kharka
fresh (vegetables)	lyan·lyah	llanlla
greasy/fatty	wee·rah·sah·pah	wirasapa
to heat	k'o·nyee·chee	q'uñichiy
hot (temperature)	k'o·nyee	q'uñi
increase/addition	yah·pah	yapa
meat	(see·k'ah) ai·chah	(siq'a) aycha
raw	hahn·kool/chah·wah	hanku/chawa
to salt	kah·chee·chai	kachichay
salty	kah·chee·sah·pah	kachisapa
sour	p'os·ko	p'usqu
spicy	hah·yah	haya
stale/spoiled	mah·k'ah	maq'a
sweet	mees·k'ee	misk'i
to sweeten	mees·k'ee·chee	misk'ichiy
tart	k-hahkh·tee/lyo·ke	qhaqti/lluqi
to taste	mah·lyee	malliy
thick	t-hah·kah	thaka
watery	yah·koo·sah·pah	yakusapa

ANDEAN COOK-OUTS

In many rural regions, midday meals for special occasions and celebrations are still prepared in a cooking pit, or *pachamanka*, pah·chah·*mahn*·kah. A hole is dug and a small 'house' of stones constructed over it. A fire is built inside the 'house', heating the stones until they're white-hot, at which point they're tumbled into the hole. Meats, tubers, vegetables, tamales (meat parcels), grains and herbs are sandwiched between the layers of hot rock. Finally, the oven is sealed shut with herbs and large leaves to keep soil from falling through into the food, and covered with earth to seal in the heat until it's cooked to perfection. Meals are served sitting in a circle on the ground and are eaten as finger food.

FOOD

ANDEAN STAPLE DISHES   LLAQTANCHISPA MIKHUNAN

These are typical dishes that tend to be served every day, with little variation. Each region has its specialities but some dishes are common throughout the Andes:

chokh·lyo wai·k'oo   *chuqllu wayk'u*
corn on the cob – available from March through to May, it's boiled and served with a kind of unripened cheese

choo·pee   *chupi*
soup made from a variety of regional ingredients

ch'oo·nyoo   *ch'uñu*
dried potatoes, *ch'arki*, *ch'ahr·kee*, and dried meat – similar to jerky – prepared with aromatic herbs

hah·k'oo/mahch·kah   *hak'u/machka*
a flour made of any of a variety of grains (wheat, barley, quinoa or *cañihua*; or dried beans or peas)

hahn·k'ah/hahm·kah/   *hank'a/hamka/kamcha*
kahm·chah
popcorn made from large kernels and served with a dry, cheddar-like cheese. The corn is toasted – or 'popped' – inside a *k'allana*, *k'ah·lyah·nah*, a low, open clay pot, and is put inside a clay oven known as a *q'uncha*, *k'on·chah*, or *tullpa*, *tooly·pah*

moo·tee   *mut'i*
dried corn kernels, boiled. A part of every corn harvest is set aside for drying, to be added to soup or ground into flour.

oo·choo koo·tah   *uchu kuta*
hot pepper paste, that accompanies varieties of tuber

p·hoos·poo/poos·poo   *phuspu/puspu*
dried beans (though can be fresh in season) reconstituted by boiling. All boiled foods are prepared in a clay pot known as a *manka*, *mahn·kah*

FOOD

REGIONAL SPECIALITIES   WAKIN LLAQTAKUNAQ MIKHUNAN

Note the Spanish influence in the names of many dishes.

Argentina

em·pah·*nah*·dahs   *empanadas* (Spanish)
  puff pastries filled with minced meat and spices and
  other ingredients served with *ruqru, rokh·*roo, a stew

Bolivia

ch'oo·nyoo   *ch'uñu*
  freeze-dried potatoes, soaked overnight and then
  boiled to accompany main dishes

em·pah·*nah*·dahs   *empanadas salteñas* (Spanish)
sahl·*te*·nyahs
  a type of meat pie

hahly·pah·*wai*·kah   *hallpawayka*
  sauce made from tomatoes, fresh peppers and herbs

pe·*kah*·nah   *pecana* (Spanish)
  traditional Christmas dish of beef or veal cooked in
  wine and herbs

pee·ke mah·*cho*   *pique macho* (Spanish)
  beef grilled with hot peppers, chopped potatoes and
  onions and served with fried potatoes and gravy, or
  with *saqta de pollo*

sahkh·tah de *po*·lyo   *saqta de pollo*
  chicken stew with peppers and onions

seel·*pahn*·cho   *silpancho cochabambino*
co·chah·bahm·*bee*·no
  meat and egg dish covered with hot sauce

teem·poo   *timpu*
  lamb stew

troo·chah   *trucha*
  trout, a Lake Titicaca speciality

toon·tah   *tunta*
  a type of freeze-dried potato, paler than the *ch'uñu*

Colombia

hoo·*meen·*t'ah   *humint'a*
   pork, vegetable and rice tamale, wrapped in banana
   leaves and steamed
*ko·*wee   *quwi*
   grilled guinea pig

Ecuador

*cahl·*do de *pah·*tahs   *caldo de patas* (Spanish)
   soup made with cow hooves
se·*vee·*che de cah·mah·*ron   *ceviche de camarón*
   a type of shrimp cocktail   (Spanish)
free·*tah·*dah   *fritada* (Spanish)
   small pieces of fried pork, served with *muti*, fried
   bananas, potatoes and hot peppers
lyah·peen·*gah·*choo   *llapingachu*
   potato-based dish, like a potato pancake
*lo·*cro de *pah·*pah   *locro de papa*
   potato and cheese soup
*po·*lyo seen *po·*lyo   *pollo sin pollo* (Spanish)
   'chicken without chicken', a vegetarian dish common
   to Quito, Otavalo and Baños
*se·*co de *chee·*vo   *seco de chivo* (Spanish)
   goat stew served with rice

Peru

Ancash
*hah·*kah *chahs·*kee   *haka chaski*
   guinea pig soup
*pah·*pah *chahs·*kee   *papa chaski*
   potato soup made with milk and cottage cheese
pe·*cahn cahl·*do   *pecán caldo* (Spanish)
   lamb's head broth
*roo·*roo *hee·*lyee   *ruru hilli*
   fruit punch made with local seasonal fruits

wahly·pah chahs·kee   *wallpa chaski*
  chicken broth with peanuts and almonds
yoo·kah shoo·pee   *yuka shupi*
  low-fat soup served the morning after a late night

Arequipa
choo·pee de cah·mah·ro·nes   *chupi de camarones*
  prawn soup
pahn·kah oo·choo   *panka uchu*
  a special form of the ever-present ground hot pepper
ro·co·to re·lye·no   *rocoto relleno* (Spanish)
  a variety of stuffed hot peppers

Ayacucho
ah·roo·woo   *aruwu*
  meat stew (most often pork)
chee·chah·roo   *chicharu*
  fried shredded pork and potatoes
kahn·kah   *kanka*
  roast beef sauteed with onions, garlic, hot peppers
  and spices
moon·doon·goo   *mundungu*
  thick, rich soup made with beef, lamb or pork, usually
  including the tripe
pah·tah·chee   *patachi*
  thick soup made with barley and bacon
poo·chee·roo/teem·poo   *puchiru/timpu*
  thick soup of varying meats, tubers, legumes and rice
poo·kah pee·kahn·tee   *puka pikanti*
  spicy stew based on potatoes, sugar beets and
  peanuts, usually served on rice
ko·wee kahn·kah   *quwi kanka*
  fried guinea pig

FOOD

Cuzco

chee·ree oo·choo   *chiri uchu*
a spicy dish of fried meat and hot peppers, especially popular during the Corpus Christi festival

lo·mo   *lomo* (Spanish)
fried beef prepared with onions, tomatoes, rice, potatoes, and a unique blend of seasonings

pah·ko·chah/   *paqucha/*
ahl·pah·kah ai·chah   *alpaka aycha*
alpaca meat

pe·pyahn de kui   *pepián de cuy* (Spanish)
fried rabbit or guinea pig served with rice and/or boiled potatoes

poo·chee·roo/teem·po   *puchiru/timpu*
soup of steak, lamb's head, bacon and raisins, often including cabbage, potatoes, chickpeas and rice

troo·chah   *trucha*
trout

Puno

kahn·kah·choo   *kankachu*
roast suckling pig, veal or lamb, prepared with hot peppers, ground spices, white wine, lemon, garlic, oil and pureed papaya

kah·rah·chee teem·poo   *karachi timpu*
thick fish stew made with *karachi*, kah·rah·chee (a fish from Lake Titicaca), *muña*, moo·nyah (an aromatic herb), *ch'uñu*, *ch'oo·nyoo*, garlic, onion and hot peppers

ke·so oo·mah·chah   *queso umacha*
stew made with hot peppers, farmers' cheese, diced onion, milk and eggs, served over boiled potatoes

AT THE MARKET   QHATUPI

Where can I find the ...?
    mai·*pee*·tahkh ... kahn?   ¿*Maypitaq ... kan?*
I want to buy some ...
    ...tah rahn·*tee*·tah moo·*nah*·nee   *...-ta rantiyta munani.*

Meat & Poultry   Imaymana Aychakuna

beef	*wah*·kah *ai*·chah	waka aycha
chicken	*wahly*·pah *ai*·cha	wallpa aycha
dried meat/jerky	*ch'ahr*·kee	ch'arki
duck	*pah*·too *ai*·chah	patu aycha
eggs	*roon*·too	runtu
fat/grease	*wee*·rah	wira
goat	*kah*·brah *ai*·chah	kabra aycha
guinea pig	*ko*·wee *ai*·chah	quwi aycha
lamb	oo·*wee*·hah *ai*·chah	uwiha aycha
llama	*lyah*·mah *ai*·chah	llama aycha
meat	*ai*·chah	aycha
partridge	*lyoo*·t-hoo/	lluthu/
	yoo·too *ai*·chah	yutu aycha
pork	k-*hoo*·chee *ai*·chah	khuchi aycha
pork rind	k-*hoo*·chee *kah*·rahn	khuchi qaran
rabbit	*ko*·wee *ai*·chah	quwi aycha
ribs	*wahkh*·tah *ai*·chah	waqta aycha
tripe	*ch'oon*·chool	ch'unchul
turkey	*pah*·woo *ai*·chah	pawu aycha

Vegetables   Mikhuna Qurakuna

cabbage	*koo*·lees	kulis
capsicum	pee·*meen*·tah	piminta
carrot	sah·*noor*·yah	sanurya
corn kernels	wee·*nyah*·poo	wiñapu
corn (on the cob)	*chokh*·lyo ee·*lyah*·koo	chuqllu illaku
fava beans	*hah*·wahs	hawas
garlic	*ah*·hoos	ahus
hot pepper	ro·*ko*·to/oo·choo	ruqutu/uchu
lettuce	lee·*choo*·gah	lichuga

FOOD

onions (spring)	see·*wee*·lyah	*siwilla*
peas	ahl·*weer*·hahs	*alwirhas*
potato	*pah*·pah	*papa*
pumpkin	sah·*pah*·lyoo	*sapallu*
tomato	too·*mah*·tee	*tumati*

THE DIVINE POTATO

Andean legend relates that when the first Inca ruler *Manqu Khapaq* and his consort *Mama Uqllu* emerged from Lake Titicaca to found their empire, the first thing their god, *Wiraqucha*, wee·rah·*ko*·chah, did was to teach them to plant potato fields.

Andeans name new potato varieties in creative ways to reflect their shape, flavour and texture. The popular yellow potato is known as *runtu papa*, *roon*·too *pah*·pah: *runtu* is the Quechua word for 'egg', and this potato has similar qualities to a hard-boiled egg. Other names are equally evocative, such as the *yana ñawi*, *yah*·nah *nyah*·wee, or 'black-eyed potato', and the *q'uyu tawna*, *k'o*·yoo *tow*·nah, or 'purple walking cane'. There are nearly 4000 varieties of potato to be found in its place of origin, the Andes.

Pulses, Grains & Legumes   Ch'aki Rurukuna

barley	see·*wah*·rah	*siwara*
bread	t'ahn·tah	*t'anta*
cañihua	kah·*nyee*·wah	*qañiwa*
dried beans	poo·*roo*·too	*purutu*
flour	*hah*·k'o	*hak'u*
kiwicha	kee·*wee*·chah	*kiwicha*
maize (dried corn)	*sah*·rah	*sara*
quinoa	*kyoo*·nyah/*kyoo*·nah	*kiwña/kiwna*
red and black bean	wai·*roo*·roo	*wayruru*
rice	*ah*·roos	*arus*
turnip (wild)	*yoo*·yoo	*yuyu*
wheat	*tree*·yoo	*triyu*

Fruit
Ruru

apple	mahn·*sah*·nah	*mansana*
avocado	*pahl*·tah	*palta*
banana	lah·*tah*·noos	*latanus*
fruit	*roo*·roo	*ruru*
medlar	nees·*pee*·roos/	*nispirus/*
(like crabapple)	wees·*wee*·roos	*wiswirus*
orange	lah·*rahn*·hah	*laranha*
peach	doo·*rahs*·noo	*durasnu*
sour cherry	kah·*poo*·lee/*reen*·dahs	*kapuli/rindas*
tumbo fruit	*teen*·teen	*tintin*

Dairy Products
Lichimanta Mikhuykuna

butter	mahn·tee·*kee*·lyah	*mantikilla*
cheese	*kee*·soo	*kisu*
milk	*lee*·chee	*lichi*

Spices & Condiments
Misk'ipakuna

chillies/hot pepper	*oo*·choo	*uchu*
cinnamon	kah·*nee*·lah	*kanila*
coriander *(cilantro)*	koo·*lahm*·troo	*kulantru*
garlic	*ah*·hoos	*ahus*
honey	lah·*chee*·wah/	*lachiwa/*
	ah·*nyah*·kah	*añaka*
huacatay	wah·*kah*·tai	*wakatay*
(aromatic herb)		
oil	ah·*see*·tee	*asiti*
parsley	pee·*ree*·heel	*pirihil*
pepper	pee·*meen*·tah	*piminta*
salt	*kah*·chee	*kachi*
sauce (of tomato	*oo*·choo *koo*·tah	*uchu kuta*
and hot pepper)		
sugar	mees·k'ee/ah·*soo*·kahr	*misk'i/asukar*

DRINKS
Nonalcoholic

UKYANAKUNA
Ukyana

Every region has its typical fruit juices such as the *likwarus,* leek·*wah*·roos, 'fruit shakes', of Bolivia, widely available in cities. Soft drinks are rare but not impossible to find in rural areas, particularly during festivals and fairs. They're considered a great luxury for the highlanders, who usually drink herbal tea. One variety is *chicha (aqhalaha,* ah·k-hah/*ah*·hah, in Quechua) made from quinoa instead of corn.

chicha morada (made from purple corn)	koo·lyee *ah*·k-hah/*ah*·hah	*kulli aqhalaha*
coca leaf tea	*koo*·kah *mah*·tee	*kuka mati*
coffee	*kah*·fee	*kaphiy*
cold water	*chee*·ree oo·noo/*yah*·koo	*chiri unu/yaku*
corn tea (Bolivian)	*ah*·pee	*api*
(in Peru, *api* is purple cornstarch pudding)		
herbal tea	*ko*·rah oo·noo	*qura unu*
hot water	*k'o*·nyee oo·noo/*yah*·koo	*q'uñi unu/yaku*
juice	*hee*·lyee	*hilli*
lemonade	lee·moo·*nah*·rah	*limunara*
mineral water	woo·tee·*lyah*·pee oo·noo	*wutillapi unu*
soda/soft drink	*koo*·lah/gah·see·*yoo*·sah	*kula/gasiyusa*
tea ...	tee ...	*tiy* ...
with milk	lee·chee·*yokh*·tah	*lichiyuqta*
without milk	*mah*·nah lee·chee·*yokh*·tah	*mana lichiyuqta*
with sugar	mees·k'ee·*yokh*·tah; ah·soo·kahr·nee·*yokh*·tah	*misk'iyuqta asukarniyuqta*
without sugar	*mah*·nah mees·k'ee·*yokh*·tah; *mah*·nah ah·soo·kahr·nee·*yokh*·tah	*mana misk'iyuqta; mana asukarniyuqta*
toasted barley tea	see·*wah*·rah oo·noo	*siwara unu*
water	oo·noo/*yah*·koo	*unu/yaku*

THE ANDEAN WONDER DRINK

The coca leaf has a long tradition of sacred and medicinal use in Andean cultures. It's most commonly chewed, or brewed as a tea, *kuka mati,* **koo·kah mah·tee**. The tea is prepared by pouring boiling water directly over the coca leaves, or by using coca tea bags which can be bought in any grocery store.

Coca's medicinal uses have been well documented. It's perhaps best known for its energising properties when one is hungry and tired, and for its ability to combat altitude sickness. Perhaps less well known by foreigners, but definitely appreciated by the locals, is its ability to aid digestion, cure diarrhoea and ease labour pains!

Alcoholic   **Waqtu**

Every region has its own special beers, wines and cocktails. Peru is known for *pisco,* **pees·**ko, a strong brandy distilled from grapes. *Chicha* or *aqha/aha,* **ah·**k-hah/*ah·*hah, is traditional corn beer, prepared and drunk throughout the Andean countries for centuries. *Singani,* **seen·gah·**nee, is a Bolivian drink made from a by-product of wine-making, mixed with lemon juice, lemon soda and ice.

beer	**seer·**wee**·sah**	*sirwisa*
brandy	*trah·***woo**	*trawu*
chicha (maize beer)	*ah·*k-hah/*ah·*hah	*aqha/aha*
chicha bar	*ah·*k-hah *wah·*see	*aqha wasi*
singani	**seen·***gah·***nee**	*singani*

Any health care in the high, remote Andes is likely to take place with a *hampiq*, **hahm**·pekh, 'healer' (or *curandero/a* (m/f) in Spanish), instead of a medical doctor. Healers use traditional folk medicine based on herbs, stones, potions and animal fats. Carry your own medicines or first aid kit with you when you're travelling, just to be on the safe side.

In metropolitan areas and populous regions, you'll always be able to find medical services. These places will operate in Spanish, as will the staff at the medical posts scattered few and far between in rural areas.

See Trekking, page 112, for advice on altitude sickness.

Is there a ...	*kahn*·choo ...	*¿Kanchu ...*
around here?	*kai*·pee?	*kaypi?*
chemist/ pharmacy	hahm·*pee*·yokh *wah*·see	*hampiyuq wasi*
dentist	*kee*·roo *see*·k'ekh	*kiru sik'iq*
doctor	mee·*dee*·koo/*dook*·toor	*midiku/duktur*
healer	*hahm*·pekh	*hampiq*
hospital	hahm·*pee*·nah *wah*·see	*hampina wasi*

WITH THE HEALER   HAMPIQWAN

Could the healer come here?
  pahkh·tah hahm·*pekh*·kah
  kai·mahn hah·moo·*rui*·mahn?

¿Paqta hampiqqa kayman hamurquyman?

I'm sick.
  on·ko·*shah*·neen

Unqushanin.

My friend is sick.
  rekh·see·nah·kokh·*mah*·see
  on·*ko*·shahn

Riqsinakuqmasiy unqushan.

I have a toothache.
  kee·*rui*·mee nah·nah·*wah*·shahn

Kiruymi nanawashan.

HEALTH

I've broken my tooth.
    kee·*rui*·mee p'ah·*kee*·roon   *Kiruymi p'akirqun.*
My mouth hurts.
    see·*mee*·mee nah·nah·*wah*·shahn   *Simiymi nanawashan.*

Ouch!   **ah·chah·*kow*!**   *¡Achakáw!*

AILMENTS   UNQUYKUNA

I feel nauseous.
    mee·lyah·nah·yah·wah·   *Millanayawashanmi/*
    shahn·mee/
    wees·ch'oo·nah·yah·wah·   *Wisch'unayawashanmi.*
    shahn·mee
I feel under the weather.
    mah·nahn ah·*lyeen*·choo   *Manan allinchu*
    kah·*shah*·nee   *kashani.*
I feel weak.
    mah·nah kahly·pah·*yokh*·mee   *Mana kallpayuqmi*
    kah·*shah*·nee   *kashani.*
I'm ill.
    on·ko·*shah*·neen   *Unqushanin.*

THE HEALER MAY SAY ...

ee·mah·nah·*soon*·keen?   *¿Imanasunkin?*
    What's the matter?

ee·mai·lyai·*kee*·pahs   *¿Imallaykipas*
nah·nah·soon·*kee*·choo?   *nanasunkichu?*
    Do you feel any pain?

mai·peen nah·nah·   *¿Maypin nanasunki?*
soon·kee?
    Where does it hurt?

e·*mai*·keen nah·nah·   *¿Imaykin nanasunki?*
soon·kee?
    What part of your body hurts?

THE HEALER MAY SAY ... (cont.)

roo·p-hai
on·koi·*wahn*·choo
kah·*shahn*·kee?
  Do you have a temperature?

¿Ruphay
unquywanchu
kashanki?

hai·k'ah p'oon·*chai*·nyahn
on·ko·*shahn*·kee?
  How long have you been like this?

¿Hayk'a p'unchayñan
unqushanki?

k'ee·koo·chee·koo·
shahn·*kee*·choo?;
yah·wahr·nee·*kee*·choo
hah·*moo*·shan?
  Are you menstruating?

¿K'ikuchikushankichu?;
¿Yawarniykichu
hamushan?

week·sah·*yokh*·choo
kah·*shahn*·kee?
  Are you pregnant?

¿Wiksayuqchu
kashanki?

kai *(k'o*·nyee) koo·kah
mah·*tee*·tah ook·yah·
kui·kui
  Drink this cup of (hot) coca leaf tea.

Kay (q'uñi) kuka
matita ukyakuykuy.

no·kahn
hahm·pee·roo·*sai*·kee
  I'll cure your illness.

Nuqan
hampirqusayki.

ah·mah lyah·kee·*kui*·choo,
koo·nah·chah·*lyahn*·mee
ah·*lyeen*·*yahn*·kee
  Don't worry, you'll get well soon.

Ama llakikuychu,
kunachallanmi
allinyanki.

ah·*lyee*·choo ...	*Allichu* ...	Please ... here.
kai·pee	*kaypi.*	
see·*ree*·kui	*sirikuy*	lie down
tee·*yah*·kui	*tiyakuy*	sit down
poo·*nyoo*·kui	*puñukuy*	sleep
sah·*mah*·kui	*samakuy*	rest

HEALTH

It hurts here.
    kai·pee nah·nah·*wah*·shahn   *Kaypi nanawashan.*
I feel better/worse.
    ah·lyeen·yah·*shah*·neen/   *Allinyashanin/*
    seen·cheer·ko·*shah*·neen   *Sinchirqushanin.*
I've been vomiting for (two days).
    (ees·kai p'oon·*chai*·nyahn)   *(Iskay p'unchayñan)*
    week·ch'oo·pah·*koo*·nee   *wikch'upakuni.*
I can't sleep.
    mah·nahn poo·*nyui*·tah   *Manan puñuyta*
    ah·tee·*nee*·choo   *atinichu.*

I burned myself.
    roo·p·hah·chee·koo·*roo*·neen   *Ruphachikurqunin.*
I've been bitten by a
dog/snake/insect.
    ahl·ko/mah·*ch'ahkh*·wai/   *Alqu/Mach'aqway/*
    koo·roo kah·nee·*roo*·wahn   *Kuru kanirquwan.*
I've sprained my wrist/ankle.
    mah·kee/*chah*·kee mo·*koy*·tahn   *Maki/Chaki muquytan*
    k'e·wee·koo·*roo*·nee   *q'iwikurquni.*
I think I have worms.
    week·*sai*·pee koo·roo·*yokh*·choos   *Wiksaypi kuruyuqchus*
    hee·nah kah·*shah*·nee   *hina kashani.*
I have a rash.
    k·*hee*·kee on·koy·*wahn*·mee   *Khiki unquywanmi*
    kah·*shah*·nee   *kashani.*

HEALTH

I feel ...	...·*wahn*·mee	...-*wanmi*
	kah·*shah*·nee	*kashani.*
dizzy	*oo*·mah *moo*·yui	*uma muyuy*
shivery	k-hah·*tah*·tai	*khatatay*

I have (a/an) ...	...·*wahn*·mee	...-*wanmi*
	kah·*shah*·nee	*kashani.*
altitude sickness	soo·*roo*·chee	*suruchi*
bronchitis	*nee*·shoo *oo*·hoo	*nishu uhu*
chickenpox	sah·rahn·*pee*·yoon	*saranpiyun*
cold	*chee*·ree *on*·koy	*chiri unquy*
constipation	*ah*·kah *k'ees*·kee	*aka k'iski*
cough	*oo*·hoo	*uhu*
diarrhoea	*k'e*·chah *on*·koy	*q'icha unquy*
fever	*roo*·p-hai *on*·koy	*ruphay unquy*
fleas	*pee*·kee	*piki*
headache	*oo*·mah *nah*·nai	*uma nanay*
influenza	*ch-hoo*·lyee/	*chhulli/*
	hah·ch'ee	*hach'i*
lice	oo·sah·*koo*·nah	*usakuna*
lump	*k'om*·poo	*q'umpu*
malaria	*chookh*·choo *on*·koy	*chukchu unquy*
migraine	*nee*·shoo	*nishu*
	oo·mah *nah*·nai	*uma nanay*
rash	k-hee·kee/k-*heer*·kee	*khiki/khirki*
sore throat	*ton*·kor *nah*·nai	*tunqur nanay*
stomachache	*week*·sah *nah*·nai	*wiksa nanay*
sunburn	*roo*·p-hai	*ruphay*
toothache	*kee*·roo *nah*·nai	*kiru nanay*
urinary tract	*hees*·p'ai *p'ee*·tee/	*hisp'ay p'iti/*
infection	*on*·koy	*unquy*
wound	*k'ee*·ree	*k'iri*

HEALTH

WOMEN'S HEALTH

WARMIKUNAQ QHALI KAYNIN

Could I see a female healer?
  *pahkh·tah warh·mee
  hahm·pekh·wahn
  hahm·pee·chee·kui·mahn?*

*¿Paqta warmi
hampiqwan
hampichikuyman?*

I'm pregnant.
  week·sah·yokh·mee kah·nee

Wiksayuqmi kani.

I think I'm pregnant.
  *week·sah·yoos·choos
  hee·nah kah·shah·nee*

*Wiksayuschus
hina kashani.*

I haven't had my period
for ... weeks.
  *...nyah yah·wahr·nee mah·nah
  hah·moon·choo*

*...-ña yawarniy mana
hamunchu.*

SPECIAL HEALTH NEEDS

UNQUQKUNA QHALI KANANPAQ

I have ...   *...wahn·mee kah·shah·nee*   *...-wanmi kashani.*
  anaemia   *ah·nee·mee·yah*   *animiya*
  asthma   *chah·k'ee oo·hoo*   *chak'i uhu*
  epilepsy   *wah·nyui on·koy*   *wañuy unquy*
  rheumatism   *too·lyoo nah·nai*   *tullu nanay*

I suffer from allergies.
  ah·leer·hee·koon kah·nee

Alirhikun kani.

I have a weak heart.
  mah·nahn ah·lyeen·choo son·koy

Manan allinchu sunquy.

I can't see very well.
  *mah·nahn ah·lyeen·tah
  ree·kui·tah ah·tee·nee·choo*

*Manan allinta
rikuyta atinichu.*

HEALTH

PARTS OF THE BODY   AYCHA KURKU KUNU

My ... hurts.

   ...ee/·nee nah·nah·*wah*·shahn   ...-y/-niy nanawashan.

My ... is swollen.

   ...ee/·nee poon·*kees*·kah   ...-y/-niy punkisqa
   kah·shahn   kashan.

I can't move my ...

   mah·nahn ....·ee·tah/·*nee*·tah   Manan ...-ytal-niyta
   koo·yoo·*chee*·tah   kuyuchiyta
   ah·tee·*nee*·choo   atinichu.

FIX IT

Remember, when using the -y/-niy or -yta/-niyta suffixes
with words, choose the -y or -yta ending when the root
word ends in a vowel, and the -niy or -niyta ending
when it ends in a consonant.

---

ankle	*chah*·kee mo·*k-ho*·choo	chaki muqhuchu
arm	*mah*·keel/*mahr*·k'ah	maki/marq'a
back	*wah*·sah	wasa
bladder	*hees*·p'ai *poo*·roo	hisp'ay puru
bone	*too*·lyoo	tullu
bottom	*see*·kee	siki
breast	*nyoo*·nyoo	ñuñu
buttock	*see*·kee *pah*·pahn	siki papan
cheek	*k'ahkh*·lyah	k'aklla
chest	*k-hahs*·ko	qhasqu
ear	*reen*·reel/*neen*·ree	rinri/ninri
elbow	*k'oo·koo*·choo/	k'ukuchu/
	koo·choos	kuchus
eye	*nyah*·wee	ñawi
face	*oo*·yah	uya
finger	*roo*·k'ah/*ree*·roo	ruk'a/riru
foot	*chah*·kee	chaki
forehead	*mah*·t'ee	mat'i

HEALTH

hand	mah·kee	maki
head	oo·mah	uma
heart	son·ko	sunqu
hip	see·kee pah·tah	siki pata
jaw/chin	k'ah·kee	k'aki
kidney	roo·roon; wah·sah roo·roon	rurun; wasa rurun
knee	mo·ko/kon·kor	muqu/qunqur
leg	chah·kah	chaka
lips	weer·p'ah	wirp'a
liver	koo·koo·peen/ k'eep·chahn	kukupin/ k'ipchan
lungs	sor·k'ahn	surq'an
mouth	see·mee	simi
nail	see·lyoo	sillu
neck	koon·kah	kunka
nose	sen·kah	sinqa
penis	pee·chee·koo/pees·ko	pichiku/pisqu
rib	wahkh·tah	waqta
shoulder	reek·rah	rikra
skin	kah·rah	qara
spine	wah·sah too·lyoo	wasa tullu
stomach	week·sah	wiksa
teeth	kee·roo	kiru
tongue	kah·lyoo	qallu
throat	ton·kor/ton·ko·ree/ k'ah·sah	tunqur/tunquri/ q'asa
vagina	rah·k-hah	rakha
vein	seer·k'ah	sirk'a
waist	we·kow	wiqaw
wrist	mah·kee mo·ko	maki muqu

PACHAKUNAPAS RAYMIKUNAPAS
TIME, DATES & FESTIVALS

Time is flexibly defined in the Andes. While 'clock time' certainly exists, Andeans have set their schedules by the movement of the sun for centuries, and their ways of expressing the passing of time reflect this.

Despite the hard life of rural Andeans – or perhaps because of it – they find many reasons to celebrate. Weddings, baptisms, national and regional holidays, Carnival, Catholic holy days, patron saints' days and other traditional religious occasions are all reasons to take a break from work for a few hours or days.

TELLING THE TIME   URAMANTA RIMAY

Telling the time in Quechua is easy. To express the time in hours, you simply use the number for that hour, followed by *urasmi*, oo·*rahs*·mee:

It's (one) o'clock.
  (hokh) oo·*rahs*·mee   *(Huq) urasmi.*

To express the half hour, you add 'half', *kuskanniyuqmi*, koos·*kahn*·nee·*yokh*·mee, into the hour:

Half past one.
  hokh oo·rahs   *Huq uras kuskanniyuqmi.*
  koos·*kahn*·nee·*yokh*·mee

For any time between the hour and the half hour, you need to express how many minutes are added to the previous hour:

Quarter past one.
  hokh oo·rahs *choon*·kah   *Huq uras chunka*
  pees·*kah*·yokh   *pisqayuq*
  mee·noo·too·*yokh*·mee   *minutuyuqmi.*

TIME, DATES & FESTIVALS

What's the time?
ee·mah oo·rahs·mee kah·shahn?   ¿Ima urasmi kashan?

It's twenty past three.
keen·sah oo·rahs ees·kai   Kinsa uras iskay
choon·kah pees·kah·yokh   chunka pisqayuq
mee·noo·too·yokh·mee   minutuyuqmi.

Likewise, time between the half hour and the hour to come is expressed by how many minutes are lacking until the next full hour:

It's quarter to four.
choon·kah pees·kah·yokh   Chunka pisqayuq
mee·noo·too p·hahl·tahn   minutu phaltan
tah·wah oo·rahs·pahkh   tawa uraspaq.

DAYS OF THE WEEK   P'UNCHAYKUNA

Monday	*loo·*nees	lunis
Tuesday	*mahr·*tees	martis
Wednesday	meer·*koo·*lees	mirkulis
Thursday	*hui·*wees	huywis
Friday	*weer·*nees	wirnis
Saturday	sah·*wah·*roo	sawaru
Sunday	doo·*meen·*goo	dumingu

MONTHS   KILLAKUNA

January	ee·*nee·*roo *kee·*lyah	iniru killa
February	p·hyoo·*ree·*roo *kee·*lyah	phiwriru killa
March	*mahr·*soo *kee·*lyah	marsu killa
April	*ow·*reel *kee·*lyah	awril killa
May	*mah·*yoo *kee·*lyah	mayu killa
June	hoo·*nee·*yoo *kee·*lyah	huniyu killa
July	hoo·*lee·*yoo *kee·*lyah	huliyu killa
August	ah·*woos·*too *kee·*lyah	awustu killa

September	see·*teem*·ree *kee*·lyah	*sitimri killa*
October	ook·*too*·ree *kee*·lyah	*uktuwri killa*
November	noo·*weem*·bree *kee*·lyah	*nuwimbri killa*
December	dee·*seem*·ree *kee*·lyah	*disimri killa*

SEASONS

autumn	*po*·koy *mee*·t'ah	*puquy mit'a*
spring	*chee*·row *mee*·t'ah	*chiraw mit'a*
summer	*roo*·p-hai *mee*·t'ah	*ruphay mit'a*
winter	*chee*·ree *mee*·t'ah	*chiri mit'a*
dry season	*ch'ah*·kee *mee*·t'ah	*ch'aki mit'a*
rainy season	*pah*·rah *mee*·t'ah	*para mit'a*

MIT'AKUNA

TIME, DATES & FESTIVALS

BY THE SUN ...

In areas where people don't own watches, they tell the time by the sun's movements.

inti siqay;   *een·tee se·kai;*
inti lluqsimuy   *een·tee lyokh·see·mui*
   dawn/sunrise ('the sun comes up')

inti llipipimuy   *een·tee lyee·pee·pee·mui*
   sunrise ('flickering sun')

inti t'iksuy;   *een·tee t'eek·sui;*
qhata inti   *k-hah·tah een·tee*
   late afternoon ('the sun leans'/'sloping sun')

inti haykuy   *een·tee hai·kui*
   sunset (sundown/'the sun goes down behind
   the horizon')

intiq lluqsinan   *een·tekh llokh·see·nahn*
   east ('where the sun comes up')

intiq chinkanan   *een·tekh cheen·kah·nahn*
   west ('where the sun disappears')

DATES

What's the date today?
   ee·mah pah·*chah*·tahkh *koo*·nahn?
It's 18 October.
   choon·kah poo·sahkh·*nee*·yokh
   ook·*too*·ree *kee*·lyahn

PACHAKUNA

¿Ima pachataq kunan?

Chunka pusaqniyuq uktuwri killan.

Present

now	*koo*·nahn	
today	*koo*·nahn *p'oon*·chai	
tonight	ch'ee·*see*·mahn	
this ...	*koo*·nahn ...	
morning		too·tah·*mahn*·tahn
afternoon		*een*·tee teek·*sui*·pee;
		tai·*ree*·mahn
night		*too*·tah
week		see·*mah*·nah
month		*kee*·lyah
year		*wah*·tah

Kunan Pacha

kunan
kunan p'unchay
ch'isiman
kunan ...
  tutamantan
  inti t'iksuypi;
  tayriman
  tuta
  simana
  killa
  wata

Past

yesterday	*kai*·nah *p'oon*·chai	
day before	kai·*neem*·pah	
yesterday	*p'oon*·chai	
yesterday ...	*kai*·nah ...	
morning		too·tah·*mahn*·tahn
afternoon		*een*·tee
evening		t'eek·*sui*·pee/*ch'ee*·see
last ...	*kai*·nah ...	
night		*too*·tah
week		see·*mah*·nah
month		*kee*·lyah
year		*wah*·tah
since (May)	(*mah*·yoo kee·*lyah*)·	
	mahn·tah	

Qayna Pacha

qayna p'unchay
qaynimpa
p'unchay
qayna ...
  tutamantan
  inti
  t'iksuypi/ch'isi
qayna ...
  tuta
  simana
  killa
  wata
(mayu killa)-
manta

TIME, DATES & FESTIVALS

Future / Hawa Pacha

English	Pronunciation	Quechua
tomorrow ...	pah·*kah*·reen ...	paqarin ...
morning	too·tah·*mahn*·tahn	tutamantan
afternoon	*een*·tee teek·*sui*·pee; *tai*·*ree*·mahn	inti t'iksuypi; tayriman
evening	*ch'ee*·see	ch'isi
day after tomorrow	*meen*·ch-hah	minchha
next ...	*k'ah*·yah/*hah*·wah ...	q'aya/hawa ...
week	see·*mah*·nah	simana
month	*kee*·lyah	killa
year	*wah*·tah	wata
in (five) minutes	(*pees*·kah) mee·noo·too·*mahn*·tah	(pisqa) minutumanta
until (June)	(hoo·*nee*·yoo kee·*lyah*)·*kah*·mah	(huniyu killa)-kama

DURING THE DAY / P'UNCHAYPI

English	Pronunciation	Quechua
afternoon	*een*·tee *t'eek*·sui; *tai*·ree	inti t'iksuy; tayri
dawn	*een*·tee *se*·kai/ *lyokh*·see	inti siqay/ lluqsiy
day	*p'oon*·chai/*p'oon*·chow	p'unchay/p'unchaw
early	too·tah·lyah·*mahn*·tah	tutallamanta
evening	*ch'ee*·seen	ch'isin
lunchtime	mee·k-hui *oo*·rah	mikhuy ura
midday	chow·pee *p'oon*·chai	chawpi p'unchay
midnight	chow·pee *too*·tah	chawpi tuta
morning	too·tah·*mahn*·tahn	tutamantan
night	*too*·tah	tuta
noon	chow·pee *p'oon*·chai	chawpi p'unchay

TIMES, DATES & FESTIVALS

FESTIVALS & NATIONAL HOLIDAYS

RAYMIKUNAPAS HATUN P'UNCHAYKUNAPAS

The Andean countries are predominantly Catholic, and numerous holy days and ancient traditions fill the celebration calendar. Any religious event is also a social event, a reason to gather and celebrate.

Inti Raymi   *een·tee rai·mee*

The 'Festival of the Sun' honours the sun god, the highest of the Andean deities, and is a week-long celebration held during the winter solstice. The high point of the festival occurs in Sacsayhuamán, just outside of Cuzco. 24 June is the day of *Inti Raymi*, which marks the beginning of the sun's New Year. It was banned for centuries by the Catholic church, but continued to be held in secret.

Mamacha Kandilarya mah·*mah*·chah
kahn·dee·*lahr*·yah

The Festival of the Virgin of the Candelaria. She is the patron saint of both Bolivia and Peru and is known throughout South America as a worker of great miracles. Festivities in her honour – parades, music, dancing, food and drink, and an interesting mix of Andean and Catholic religious rituals – begin a week prior to 2 February. The colour and incomparable majesty of these events is a prelude to Carnival.

Karnawal kahr·*nah*·wahl

Carnival is celebrated throughout South America, but takes on a uniquely Andean flavour in Bolivia, Peru and Ecuador, where each region has its own special traditions. The week-long celebrations take place the week before Ash Wednesday on the Catholic calendar. Everyone lives it up before the fasting and sacrifice of Lent.

Día de Todos los Santos dee·ah de *to*·dos los *sahn*·tos
Día de los Muertos dee·ah de los *mwer*·tos

All Saints' Day on 1 November and All Souls' Day, the next day, are more than a simple observance honouring the saints and departed family members – they have become enmeshed with Andean beliefs and practices for honouring the dead. After attending Mass, community members prepare a feast, often served in the local cemetery so that departed family members can participate. There are always some favourite dishes – often lavishly decorated – of those who have passed away.

Nawida P'unchay nah·*wee*·dah *p'oon*·chai

Midnight Mass and street celebrations with music, dancing, food and drinks on Christmas Eve and Christmas Day are common. You'll see the nativity scene everywhere in homes and churches. In less Christian areas, Christmas may be celebrated as a harvest festival.

TIME, DATES & FESTIVALS

Año Nuevo
*ah·*nyo *nwe·*vo

New Year's Eve and New Year's Day are included in the general Christmas festivities. Regional traditions involve processions, gatherings and public dancing where everyone joins in. In some parts of Bolivia, the Christmas season celebrations last until the end of January.

Día de los Reyes Magos
*dee·*ah de los *re·*yes *mah·*gos

Epiphany, or the Feast of the Three Kings, on 6 January, marks the end of the Christmas season. It's the day children traditionally receive their Christmas gifts.

Fiestas Patrias
*fyes·*tahs *pah·*tryahs

Every Latin American country celebrates the day it achieved independence from Spain. It's a time of parties and demonstrations of patriotism, people wave flags and sing national anthems during the colourful parades. Peru's Independence Day is 28 July, Bolivia's 6 August and Ecuador's 10 August.

Día del Santo Patrón
*dee·*ah del *sahn·*to pah·*tron*

National, regional and local patron saints' days vary according to the saint being honoured. The festivities may be one to several days in length, and generally include music and dancing, as well as special Masses and services. They are as much a social event and party as a dedicated religious observance – saints' day celebrations are a treat not to be missed.

Aniversario de Fundación
ah·nee·ver·*sah·*ryo de foon·dah·*syon*

Many cities, towns and villages celebrate the anniversary of their founding. Since these are secular celebrations, there may or may not be a special Mass offered, but there'll always be typical Andean festivities.

CHRISTENINGS & WEDDINGS

ULIYAYKUNAPAS KASARAKUYKUNAPAS

Given the wide variety of traditions, weddings can be performed and celebrated in very different ways. Christenings, on the other hand, are fairly uniform due to the influence of Catholicism. They're an all-day affair, accompanied by a feast put on by the godparents. As with other celebrations, there is much singing and dancing, eating and drinking.

Congratulations!
    koo·see·*koos*·pah
    kow·sah·koon·*kee*·chees!
              ¡Kusikuspa
              kawsakunkichis!
To the bride and groom!
    kah·sah·rahkh·*koo*·nah
    how·*kah*·lyah kow·sah·*choon*·koo!
              ¡Kasaraqkuna
              hawkalla kawsachunku!

baptism	oo·lee·yoo/wow·*tee*·soo	*uliyu/wawtisu*
to baptise/ christen	oo·*lee*·yai/oo·*noo*·chai/ wow·*tee*·sai	*uliyay/unuchay/ wawtisay*
to celebrate	k'o·choo·*ree*·chee/ fees·*tee*·hai	*q'uchurichiy/ phistihay*
to celebrate (a birthday)	fees·*tah*·kui	*phistakuy*
festival	*rai*·mee	*raymi*
gift	ree·koo·*chee*·kui	*rikuchikuy*
goddaughter	ai·*hah*·rah	*ayhara*
godfather	pah·*ree*·noo	*parinu*
godmother	mah·*ree*·nah	*marina*
godparent	mahr·*k'ah*·ke	*marq'aqi*
godson	ai·*hah*·roo	*ayharu*
holiday	*hah*·toon fees·tah	*hatun phista*
party	*fees*·tah	*phista*
wedding	kahk·sah·*rah*·kui	*kasarakuy*
wedding present	kah·sah·rahkh·koo·*nah*·pahkh ree·koo·*chee*·kui	*kasaraqkunapaq rikuchikuy*

TIME, DATES & FESTIVALS

TOASTS & CONDOLENCES

ANQUSAYKUNAPAS LLAKIPAYKUNAPAS

Bon appetit!
    mees·k'ee·lyah·*tah*·nyah
    mee·*k-hoo*·kui!

¡Misk'illataña
mikhukuy!

Bon voyage!
    ah·lyeen·*lyah*·nyah poo·*ree*·kui!

¡Allinllaña purikuy!

Cheers!
    ook·yai·*koo*·soon!

¡Ukyaykusun!

Good luck!
    ah·lyeen sah·*mee*·yokh kai!

¡Allin samiyuq kay!

Hope it goes well!
    ee·*chah*·pahs roo·wahs·*kai*·kee
    ah·lyeen *kahn*·mahn!

¡Ichapas ruwasqayki
allin kanman!

What bad luck!
    ee·mah k-*hen*·chah!

¡Ima qhincha!

Never mind!
    mah·nah ee·mah·nahn·*pahs*·choo!

¡Mana imananpaschu!

Get well soon!
    oos·*k-hai*·lyah ah·lyeen·*yah*·yai!

¡Usqhaylla allinyayay!

I'm very sorry.
    ahn·*chah*·tahn lyah·kee·*pai*·kee

Anchatan llakipayki.

My deepest sympathy.
    seen·*chee*·tahn lyah·kee·*pai*·kee

Sinchitan llakipayki.

NUMBERS & AMOUNTS

The numbers from zero to 10 each have their own name. These 'basic' numbers are also used to form the numbers from 11 to 19, which are expressed as '10 with one' through to '10 with nine'. The suffix *-yuq, -yokh*, 'with', is added to the end of units, not to the tens. Forming the tens is easy too: 20 is 'two tens', 30 is 'three tens', and so on. Remember that when a number ends in a consonant, the suffix *-ni* needs to be added before the suffix *-yuq*. For example, the number 11 is formed by joining *huq* for 'one' and *chunka* for '10' – *chunka huqniyuq, choon·kah hokh·nee·yokh*.

To count from 100 onwards, you use the same system as for the numbers one to 100. Thus the number 2002 would be *iskay waranqa iskayniyuq, ees·kai wah·rahn·kah ees·kai·nee·yokh* (lit: two thousand two-with).

CARDINAL NUMBERS   IMAKAQ YUPAKUNA

0	*ch'oo·*sahkh	*ch'usaq*
1	hokh	*huq*
2	*ees·*kai	*iskay*
3	*keen·*sah	*kinsa*
4	*tah·*wah	*tawa*
5	*pees·*kah	*pisqa*
6	*sokh·*tah	*suqta*
7	*kahn·*chees	*qanchis*
8	*poo·*sakh	*pusaq*
9	*ees·*kon	*isqun*
10	*choon·*kah	*chunka*
11	*choon·*kah hokh·*nee·*yokh	*chunka huqniyuq*
12	*choon·*kah ees·kai·*nee·*yokh	*chunka iskayniyuq*

13	*choon*·kah keen·*sah*·yokh	chunka kinsayuq
14	*choon*·kah tah·*wah*·yokh	chunka tawayuq
15	*choon*·kah pees·*kah*·yokh	chunka pisqayuq
16	*choon*·kah sokh·*tah*·yokh	chunka suqtayuq
17	*choon*·kah kahn·chees·*nee*·yokh	chunka qanchisniyuq
18	*choon*·kah poo·sahkh·*nee*·yokh	chunka pusaqniyuq
19	*choon*·kah ees·kon·*nee*·yokh	chunka isqunniyuq
20	*ees*·kay *choon*·kah	iskay chunka
21	*ees*·kay *choon*·kah hokh·*nee*·yokh	iskay chunka huqniyuq
22	*ees*·kay *choon*·kah ees·kai·*nee*·yokh	iskay chunka iskayniyuq
30	*keen*·sah *choon*·kah	kinsa chunka
40	*tah*·wah *choon*·kah	tawa chunka
50	*pees*·kah *choon*·kah	pisqa chunka
60	*sokh*·tah *choon*·kah	suqta chunka
70	*kahn*·chees *choon*·kah	qanchis chunka
80	*poo*·sakh *choon*·kah	pusaq chunka
90	*ees*·kon *choon*·kah	isqun chunka
100	*pah*·chahkh	pachak
1000	wah·*rahn*·kah	waranqa
1,000,000	*hoo*·noo	hunu

ORDINAL NUMBERS   ÑIQI YUPAKUNA

To form ordinal numbers, add either *ñiqin, nye*·ken, meaning 'order' or *kaq, kahkh*, meaning 'that which is' to the cardinal number; these endings can be used interchangeably. Note that '1st' is an exception:

1st	*nyow*·pahkh kahkh	ñawpaq kaq
2nd	*ees*·kai kahkh	iskay kaq
3rd	*keen*·sah kahkh	kinsa kaq

FRACTIONS

1/2	*ees*·kai *tah*·k'ah	*iskay taq'a*
1/3	*keen*·sah *tah*·k'ah	*kinsa taq'a*
1/4	*tah*·wah *tah*·k'ah	*tawa taq'a*
3/4	*keen*·sah *tah*·wah *tah*·k'ah	*kinsa tawa taq'a*

P'AKIKUNA

AMOUNTS

HAYK'AKAKUNA

How many/much?	*hai*·k'ah?	*¿Hayk'a?*
I need ...	....*tah* moo·*mah*·nee	*...-ta munani.*
all	*lyah*·pahn/*too*·kui/lyoo	*llapan/tukuy/lliw*
(just) a little	*ahs*·lyah/*pee*·see/	*aslla/pisi/*
	chee·*kah*·lyah	*chikalla*
some/a few	wah·*kee*·lyahn/	*wakillan/*
	pee·see/*ahs*·lyah	*pisi/aslla*
enough	chai·*lyah*	*chaylla*
few	*ahs*·lyah;	*aslla;*
	ahs pee·*see*·lyah;	*as pisilla;*
	chee·kahn; *toom*·pah	*chikan; tumpa*
less	*pee*·see	*pisi*
many/much/	*ahs*·k·hah; *yoo*·pah;	*askha; yupa;*
a lot	mai *chee*·kahn;	*may chikan;*
	mai·*too*·kui	*maytukuy*
more	ahs·*tah*·wahn	*astawan*
none/nothing	*mah*·nah ee·*mah*·pahs	*mana imapas*
once	hokh *koot*·ee	*huq kuti*
plenty	*lyah*·sahkh	*llasaq*
some	*toom*·pah/*ahs*·lyah	*tumpa/aslla*
too many/much	*ahs*·k·hah/*seen*·chee/	*askha/sinchi/*
	mai·*too*·kui/*lyah*·sahkh	*maytukuy/llasaq*

NUMBERS & AMOUNTS

JUST GIVE ME ...

a bottle	hokh woo·*tee*·lyah	*huq wutilla*
a dozen	*choon*·kah	*chunka*
	ees·kai·nee·yokh·neen·teen;	*iskayniyuq-nintin;*
	hokh doo·*see*·nah	*huq dusina*
half a kilo	*meed*·yoo kee·*loo*	*midyu kilu*
half a dozen	*meed*·yah doo·*see*·nah	*midya dusina*
a kilo	wah·*rahn*·kah ahkh·noo	*waranqa-aqnu*
a hand full	*hahp-h*·t'ai	*hapht'ay*
two handfuls	*pot*·koi	*putquy*
100 grams	*pah*·chahkh-*ahkh*·noo	*pachak-aqnu*
a packet	hokh pah·*kee*·tee	*huq pakiti*
a pair	ees·kai·*neen*·teen	*iskaynintin*
a piece	*ahkh*·noo	*aqnu*
a pile	*ko*·too/*row*·k-hah/*moon*·toon/*tow*·kah	*qutu/rawkha/muntun/tawqa*

USQHAYLLAPAQÑA
EMERGENCIES

In rural and remote areas, Quechua could be vital.

Fire!	*nee*·nah roo·*p·hah*·shahn!	¡Nina ruphashan!
Go away!	*ree*·pui!;	¡Ripuy!;
	lyokh·see kai·*mahn*·tah!	¡Lluqsiy kaymanta!
Help!	yah·nah·*pah*·wai!	¡Yanapaway!
Stop!	*sah*·yai!	¡Sayay!
Thief!	*soo*·wah!	¡Suwa!
Watch out!	pahkh·*tah*·tahkh!/	¡Paqtaq!/
	ah·chah·*chow*!	¡Achacháw!

It's an emergency.
    seen·chee os·k·hai·*pahkh*·mee;   *Sinchi usqhaypaqmi;*
    nee·shoo pree·see·*sahkh*·mee   *Nishu prisisaqmi.*
Could you help us please?
    ah·*lyee*·choo yah·nah·pah·   ¿Allichu yanapa-
    wahn·kee·koo·*mahn*·choo?   wankikumanchu?
Could I please use the telephone?
    ah·*lyee*·choo tee·lee·foo·*noo*·wahn   ¿Allichu tiliphunuwan
    ree·mai·kui·*mahn*·choo?   rimaykuymanchu?
I'm lost.
    cheen·*kahs*·kahn kah·*shah*·nee;   *Chinkasqan kashani;*
    cheen·*kahs*·kahn poo·ree·*shah*·nee   *Chinkasqan purishani.*
Where are the toilets?
    mai·*pee*·tahkh hees·p'ah·*koo*·nah   ¿Maypitaq hisp'akuna
    kah·shahn?; mai·*pee*·tahkh   kashan?; ¿Maypitaq
    hees·p'ah·*kui*·mahn?   hisp'akuyman?
Call a doctor/healer!
    mee·dee·*koo*·tah/hahm·*pekh*·tah   !Midikuta/Hampiqta
    wahkh·*yah*·mui!   waqyamuy!
I'm ill.
    on·*kos*·kahn kah·*shah*·nee   *Unqusqan kashani.*
My friend is ill.
    rekh·see·nah·kokh·mah·*see*·mee   *Riqsinakuqmasiymi*
    on·*ko*·shahn   *unqushan.*

POLICE   WARDIYA

Call the police!
  wahr·dee·*yah*·tah wahkh·*yah*·mui!   ¡Wardiyata waqyamuy!
Where's the police station?
  mai·*pee*·tahkh koo·mee·sah·*ree*·yah   ¿Maypitaq kumisariya
  kah·shahn?   kashan?
I've been robbed.
  soo·wah·chee·koo·*roo*·neen   Suwachikurqunin.

My ... was/	...·*ee*·tahn soo·wah	...-ytan suwa
were stolen.	ah·*pah*·koon	apakun.
I've lost	...·*ee*·tahn	...-ytan
my ...	cheen·kah·chee·*roo*·nee	chinkachirquni.
backpack	*ke*·pee	qipi
bags	mah·lee·tai·koo·*nah*·tahn	malitaykunatan
handbag	wah·*yah*·kah/*ch'oos*·pah	wayaqa/ch'uspa
money	*kol*·ke	qulqi
papers	doo·koo·meen·tui·koo·*nah*·tahn	dukumintuy-kunatan
wallet	*kol*·ke choo·*rah*·nah/wee·lyee·*tee*·rah	qulqi churana/willitira

(not) guilty	(*mah*·nah) hoo·*chah*·yokh	(mana) huchayuq
police officer	*tai*·tah wahr·*dee*·yah	tayta wardiya
police station	koo·mee·sah·*ree*·yah	kumisariya
rape	ahl·*ko*·chai	alquchay
robbery/theft	soo·*wah*·kui	suwakuy

A

English	Pronunciation	Quechua
to be able	*ah·*tee	atiy
above	hah·*wahn*·pee	hawanpi
abroad	kah·roo *lyahkh*·tah	karu llaqta
to accept	*ui*·nee	uyniy
accident	ahkh·see·*deen*·tee	aksidinti
accommodation	kor·pah·*chah*·nah	qurpachana
ache	*nah*·nai	nanay
across (from)	cheem·*pah*·pee	chimpapi
adult	*wee*·nyai hoon·*t'ahs*·kah •	*wiñay hunt'asqa* •
	kaly·*pah*·yokh	*kallpayuq*
advice	*yoo*·yai koy	yuyay quy
to advise (inform)	*wee*·lyai	willay
to advise (counsel)	yoo·*yai*·chai	yuyaychay
aeroplane	ah·*wee*·yoon	awiyun
to be afraid	mahn·*chah*·kui	manchakuy
afterwards	chai·mahn·*tah*·tah	chaymanta
again	hokh·*mahn*·tah	huqmanta
against	*koon*·trah	kuntra
ago (a while ago)	hokh rah·*too*·nyah	huq ratuña
to agree to	oo·*yah*·kui	uyakuy
ahead	*nyow*·pahkh	ñawpaq
air	*wai*·rah	wayra
alcohol	*wahkh*·too	waqtu
all	*lyah*·pah	llapa
to allow	sah·*ke*·lyai	saqillay
almost	*yah*·kah	yaqa
alone	*sah*·pah	sapa
already	·nyah	-ña
also (interchangeable)	·pees • ·pahs	-pis • -pas
although	*chai*·pahs	chaypas
always	*pah*·sahkh koo·*tee*·lyah	pasaq kutilla
among	oo·k·*hoo*·pee	ukhupi
ancient	*nyow*·pah	ñawpa
angry	p·*hee*·nyah	phiña
another	hokh	huq
to answer	koo·*tee*·chee	kutichiy
anything	ee·mah·*lyah*·pahs	imallapas
to argue	choo·rah·*nah*·kui	churanakuy
to arrive	chai·*yai*	chayay
to ask (a question)	*tah*·pui	tapuy
to ask (for something)	mah·*nyah*·kui	mañakuy
awful	mah·*p'ah*	map'a

B

baby (human)	wah·wah	wawa
baby (animal)	oo·nyah	uña
babysitter	wah·wah k-hah·wahkh	wawa qhawaq
backpack	k'ee·pee	q'ipi
bad	mah·nah ah·lyeen	mana allin
bag (large)	wah·yah·kah	wayaqa
bag (small)	ch'oos·pah	ch'uspa
baggage	mah·lee·tah	malita
ball	pee·loo·tah	piluta
band (music)	koo·see·tui	kusituy
bank (shore)	kahn·too	kantu
baptism	oo·lee·yai	uliyay
to barter	ch-hah·lai	chhalay
basket	kah·nahs·tah	kanasta
to bathe	ahr·mah·kui	armakuy
bathroom	bah·nyoo	bañu
to be	kai	kay
to bear (put up with)	ah·tee·pai	atipay
bear (animal)	oo·koo·koo	ukuku
beautiful	soo·mahkh	sumaq
bed	poo·nyoo·nah	puñuna
bedroom	poo·nyoo·nah kwahr·too	puñuna kwartu
before (time)	nyow·pahkh·tah	ñawpaqta
to begin	kah·lyah·ree	qallariy
behind	k-he·pah	qhipa
to believe (religious)	ee·nee • ee·nyee	iniy • iñiy
below	oo·rai	uray
beside	wahkh·tahn·pee	waqtanpi
besides (furthermore)	hee·nahs·pah	hinaspa
better	ahs·wahn ah·lyeen	aswan allin
bicycle	wee·see·kee·lee·tah	wisiklita
big	hah·toon	hatun
bigger	ahs·wahn hah·toon	aswan hatun
birthday	wah·tah hoon·t'ai	wata hunt'ay
to bite (any creature)	kah·nee	kaniy
to bite (of an insect)	k'oo·tui	k'utuy
to bite (of a dog; chew off something)	k-hah·chui	khachuy
blanket	kah·tah • choo·see	qata • chusi
to bleed	yah·wahr·chai	yawarchay
blind (adj)	nyow·sah	ñawsa
blood	yah·wahr	yawar
to bloom/blossom	see·sai	sisay
blue (of eyes only)	k-ho·see	qhusi

boat	wahm·poo	wampu
body	ai·chah koor·koo	aycha kurku
book	lyoo·roo	liwru
border	sai·wah	saywa
bored/boring	ah·mees·kah	amisqa
to borrow	mah·nui·pee mah·nyai	manuypi mañay
both	ees·kai·neen	iskaynin
to bother	ch'ekh·mee	ch'iqmiy
bottle	woo·tee·lyah	wutilla
bottle opener	woo·tee·lyah kee·chah·nah	wutilla kichana
bottom (body)	see·kee	siki
boy	er·ke	irqi
boyfriend	yah·nah	yana
bread	t'ahn·tah	t'anta
to break	p'ah·kee	p'akiy
breakfast	too·tah·mahn·tah mee·k·hoo·nah	tutamanta mikhuna
breasts	nyoo·nyoo	ñuñu
to breathe	sah·mah·ree	samariy
bridge	chah·kah	chaka
to bring	ah·pah·mui	apamuy
broken	p'ah·kees·kah	p'akisqa
to build	per·kah·chai	pirqachay
building	hah·toon wah·see	hatun wasi
bull	too·roo	turu
bullfighting	too·roo pookh·lyai	turu pukllay
burn	roo·p-hai	ruphay
to burn	roo·p-hah·chee	ruphachiy
busy (employed)	roo·wah·nah·yokh	ruwanayuq
busy (no free time)	mah·nah kah·sekh	mana qasiq
but	ee·chah·kah	ichaqa
butter	mahn·tee·kee·lyah	mantikilla
to buy	rahn·tee	rantiy

C

cabbage	koo·lees	kulis
calf	oo·nyah	uña
to call (by shouting)	wahkh·yai	waqyay
to call (to name)	soo·tee·chai	sutichay
can (to be able)	ah·tee	atiy
can (of food)	lah·tah	lata
can opener	lah·tah kee·chah·nah	lata kichana
candles	bee·lah·koo·nah	bilakuna
capital city	oo·mah lyahkh·tah	uma llaqta

car	*kah*·rroo	*karru*
care	*k-hah*·wai	*qhaway*
to carry (on the back)	*k'e*·pee	*q'ipiy*
cassette	kah·*see*·tee	*kasiti*
Catholic	kah·too·*lee*·koo	*katuliku*
cave	*mah*·ch'ai	*mach'ay*
to celebrate	k'oo·*choo*·kui	*q'uchukuy*
cemetery	ah·yah p'ahm·*pah*·nah	*aya p'ampana*
ceramic	*k'ahkh*·rah	*k'akra*
chair	tee·*yah*·nah	*tiyana*
to change (become different)	hokh·nee·*rah*·yai	*huqnirayay*
to change (exchange)	kahm·*bee*·yai	*kambiyay*
to cheat	*k'o*·tui	*q'utuy*
cheese	*kee*·soo	*kisu*
chest	*k-hahs*·ko	*qhasqu*
chewing gum	*cheek*·lee	*chikli*
chicha (maize beer)	ah·hah • *ah*·k-hah	*aha* • *aqha*
chicha bar	ah·hah·*wah*·see	*ahawasi*
chicken	*wahly*·pah	*wallpa*
child	*wah*·wah	*wawa*
chocolate	*mees*·k'ee • choo·*koo*·lah·tee	*misk'i* • *chukulati*
to choose	*ahkh*·lyai	*akllay*
church	een·*lee*·sah	*inlisa*
cigarette	see·*yah*·roo	*siyaru*
cinema	*see*·nee	*sini*
city	*lyahkh*·tah	*llaqta*
clean (of objects)	*lui*·loo	*luylu*
clean (of water)	*ch'oo*·yah	*ch'uya*
to clean	*pee*·chai	*pichay*
cliff	*kah*·kah	*qaqa*
to climb	*wee*·chai	*wichay*
clock	*ree*·lookh	*riluh*
to close	*wees*·k'ai	*wisq'ay*
close (near)	*sees*·pah	*sispa*
clothes	*p'ah*·chah	*p'acha*
coat	*sah*·koo	*saku*
coast	*koos*·tah	*kusta*
to collect	*pah*·lyai	*pallay*
colour	*lyeem*·pee	*llimpi*
to come	*hah*·mui	*hamuy*
comedian	ah·see·*chee*·kokh	*asichikuq*
to comfort	kahly·pah·*chah*·ree	*kallpachariy*
to communicate	*wee*·lyai	*willay*
community	*ai*·lyoo	*ayllu*

176

community leader	hah·*mow*·t'ah	hamawt'a
constipation	k'ees·kee	k'iski
to cook	wai·k'ui	wayk'uy
corn	sah·rah	sara
corn on the cob	chokh·lyo	chuqllu
corner (outside)	k'oo·choo	k'uchu
corner (inside)	hoo·k'ee	huk'i
to cost	kwees·tai	kwistay
country (nation)	lyahkh·tah	llaqta
countryside	pahm·pah	pampa
cough	ch'oo·hoo • oo·hoo	ch'uhu • uhu
to cough	oo·hui	uhuy
to count	yoo·pai	yupay
courtyard	kahn·chah	kancha
cow	wah·kah	waka
crazy	wah·k'ah	waq'a
to cross	cheem·pai	chimpay
cross (angry)	p-hee·*nyahs*·kah	phiñasqa
crowd	tahn·tah	tanta
to cry	wah·kai	waqay
cup	sui·k'oo	suyk'u
cup (Incas ceremonial)	ke·roo	qiru
to cure	hahm·pee	hampiy
to cut	koo·chui	kuchuy

D

daily	sah·pah p'oon·chai	sapa p'unchay
damp	ho·k'o	huq'u
dance	too·sui	tusuy
to dance	too·sui	tusuy
danger	mahn·chai	manchay
dark (night)	too·tah	tuta
to get dark	too·*tah*·yai	tutayay
date of birth	wah·tah hoon·t'ai	wata hunt'ay
dawn	ee·*lyah*·ree • *rahn*·k-hee	illariy • rankhi
day	p'oon·chai	p'unchay
dead	wah·*nyoos*·kah	wañusqa
deaf	oo·pah	upa
to decide	kah·mah·*ree*·kui	kamarikuy
deep	oo·k·hoo	ukhu
delay	oo·nai	unay
to delay	oo·nai	unay
delicious	mees·k'ee	misk'i
dentist	kee·roo see·k'ekh	kiru sik'iq
to deny	mah·nahn nee	manan niy

to depart	*lyokh*·see	*lluqsiy*
descendent	*k-he*·pah *wee*·nyai	*qhipa wiñay*
desert	*ah*·ko *pahm*·pah	*aqu pampa*
to detour	*wahkh*·lyee	*waqlliy*
diarrhoea	*k'e*·chah	*q'icha*
to have diarrhoea	*k'e*·chai	*q'ichay*
to die	*wah*·nyui	*wañuy*
different	hokh·*nee*·rahkh	*huqniraq*
difficult	*sah*·sah	*sasa*
to direct	*yah*·*chah*·chee	*yachachiy*
dirty	*k-hahr*·kah	*kharka*
to disturb	*tah·koo*·ree	*takuriy*
dizzy	*oo*·mah moo·*yoos*·kah	*uma muyusqa*
to do/make	*roo*·wai	*ruway*
doctor	*dookh*·toor	*duktur*
done	roo·*wahs*·kah	*ruwasqa*
door	*poon*·koo	*punku*
to draw	se·*k'en*·chai	*siq'inchay*
dream/to dream	*mos*·k-hoy	*musqhuy*
dress	*p'ah*·chah	*p'acha*
to dress (oneself)	*p'ah·chah·lyee·*kui	*p'achallikuy*
to dress (someone else)	*p'ah·chah·lyee*·chee	*p'achallichiy*
drink/to drink	*ookh*·yai	*ukyay*
drug	*hahm*·pee	*hampi*
drugstore	*hahm·pee*·yokh *wah*·see	*hampiyuq wasi*
drum (small)	*teen*·yah	*tinya*
drum (large)	*wahn*·kahr	*wankar*
drunk	*mah*·chahkh	*machaq*
to get drunk	*mah*·chai	*machay*
dry	*ch'ah*·kee	*ch'aki*

E

each	*sah*·pah	*sapa*
early morning	*too·tah·lyah·mahn*·tah	*tutallamanta*
early afternoon	ah·*lyeen·pee*·rahkh	*allinpiraq*
to earn (money)	*tah*·ree	*tariy*
earth (soil)	*aly*·pah	*allpa*
the Earth	kay *pah*·chah	*kay pacha*
earth goddess (Mother Earth)	*pah·chah·mah*·mah	*Pachamama*
earthquake	*pah*·chah *koo*·yui	*pacha kuyuy*
east	*een*·tee lyokh·*see*·mui	*inti lluqsimuy*
easy	*fah*·seel	*phasil*

ENGLISH – QUECHUA DICTIONARY

to eat	mee·k-hui	mikhuy
to educate	yah·chah·chee	yachachiy
education	yah·chai	yachay
eggs	roon·too	runtu
to elect	ahk·lyai	akllay
electric light	loos	lus
to embarrass	p'en·kah·kui	p'inqakuy
embarrassed	p'en·kahs·kah	p'inqasqa
empire	tah·wahn·teen·soo·yoo	tawantinsuyu
empty	ch'oo·sahkh	ch'usaq
end	too·kui	tukuy
English	een·lees	inlis
to enjoy oneself	oo·sah·chee·kui	usachikuy
enough	chai·lyah·nyah	chayllaña
to enter	hai·kui	haykuy
to entertain	k'o·too·ree·chee	q'uturichiy
every	lyoo	lliw
everyone	lyoo·neen·koo	lliwninku
everything	lyah·pah	llapa
everywhere	mai·pee·pahs	maypipas
exact(ly)	k'ah·pahkh	k'apak
to exchange (products)	ch-hah·lai	chhalay
to exhibit	ree·koo·ree·chee	rikurichiy
to exist	kai	kay
to expect	soo·yai	suyay
expensive	ahn·chah chah·nee·yokh	ancha chaniyuq
to explain	yah·chah·chee	yachachiy

F

to fall	oor·mai	urmay
family	fah·mee·lyah	phamilla
famous	rekh·sees·kah	riqsisqa
far	kah·roo	karu
farm	chahkh·rah	chakra
farmer	chahkh·rah roo·nah	chakra runa
farmyard	kahn·chah	kancha
fast (movement)	p-hah·wai·lyah	phawaylla
fast (passage of time)	rah·too·lyah	ratulla
fat (grease)	wee·rah	wira
fault	hoo·chah	hucha
fava beans	hah·wahs	hawas
fear	mahn·chah·kui	manchakuy
to feed	kah·rai	qaray

to feel (sentiments)	*lyahkh*·lyai	*llakllay*
to feel (touch)	*lyah*·mee	*llamiy*
fence	*ken*·chah	*qincha*
festival	*rai*·mee	*raymi*
to fetch	poo·*sah*·mui	*pusamuy*
fever	*roo*·p-hah	*rupha*
few	*pee*·see	*pisi*
fiancé/fiancée	*oor*·pee	*urpi*
field (cultivated)	*chahkh*·rah	*chakra*
fight/to fight	ow·kah·*nah*·kui	*awqanakuy*
to fill	*hoon*·t'ai	*hunt'ay*
to find (something lost)	*tah*·ree	*tariy*
to finish	*too*·kui	*tukuy*
fire	*nee*·nah	*nina*
first	*nyow*·pahkh	*ñawpaq*
flashlight	k'ahn·*chah*·nah	*k'anchana*
flat (adj)	*p'ahl*·tah	*p'alta*
flat place	*pahm*·pah	*pampa*
flea	*pee*·kee	*piki*
flower	*t'ee*·kah	*t'ika*
flour	*hah*·k'oo	*hak'u*
to fly	p-hah·wai	*phaway*
fog	*pah*·chah p-hoo·yoo	*pacha phuyu*
to follow	*kah*·tee	*qatiy*
food	mee·*k-hoo*·nah	*mikhuna*
foreigner	*hah*·wah roo·nah	*hawa runa*
forest	*mahly*·kee *mahly*·kee	*mallki mallki*
forever	wee·nyai/*pah*·chah	*wiñaypacha*
to forget	*kon*·kai	*qunqay*
to forgive	pahm·*pah*·chai	*pampachay*
fort/fortress	poo·*kah*·rah	*pukara*
fortune teller	*wah*·tokh	*watuq*
free (at liberty)	*kes*·pee	*qispi*
free (no cost)	*yahn*·kahn	*yanqan*
to freeze	*kah*·sai	*qasay*
friend	rekh·see·nah·kokh·*mah*·see	*riqsinakuqmasi*
from	·*mahn*·tah	*-manta*

I'm from Cuzco.		
kos·ko·*mahn*·tah kah·nee		*Qusqu-manta kani.*

full (after a meal)	sahkh·*sahs*·kah	*saksasqa*
full (complete)	*hoon*·t'ah	*hunt'a*
to have fun	koo·*see*·kui	*kusikuy*
future	*hah*·mokh *pah*·chah	*hamuq pacha*

game	pookh·lyai	pukllay
garbage	k'o·pah	q'upa
garden (flower)	pow·kahr	pawqar
garden (fruit)	moo·yah	muya
garlic	ah·hoos	ahus
gate	hai·koo·nah	haykuna
to gather	pah·lyai	pallay
genuine	che·kahkh	chiqaq
to get lost	cheen·kai	chinkay
gift	ree·koo·chee·kui	rikuchikuy
girl	see·pahs	sipas
girlfriend	yah·nah·sah	yanasa
to give	koy	quy
to give birth (humans)	wah·chah·kui	wachakuy
to give birth (animals)	wah·chai	wachay
glass	kes·pee	qispi
to go	ree	riy
to go away	ree·pui	ripuy

> Get lost! Go away!
> *lyokh·see! ree·pui!*   ¡Lluqsiy! ¡Ripuy!

God	yah·yah	Yaya
gold	ko·ree	quri
good (adj)	ah·lyeen	allin

> Good afternoon.
> *wee·nahs tahr·dees*   Winas tardis.
>
> Good evening/night.
> *wee·nahs noo·chees*   Winas nuchis.
>
> Good morning.
> *wee·noos dee·yahs*   Winus diyas.
>
> Goodbye.
> *teen·koo·nahn·chees·kah·mah*   Tinkunanchiskama.

grass	k'ah·choo	q'achu
grave (tomb)	ah·yah sahn·k·hah	aya sankha
great (size)	hah·toon	hatun
great (quality)	koo·sah koo·sah	kusa kusa
to grow	wee·nyai	wiñay
guest	kor·pah	qurpa
guide (person)	nyahn·tah rekh·see·chekh	ñanta riqsichiq

H

hair (of body/animal)	*soo*·p-hoo	*suphu*
hair (of head)	*chookh*·chah	*chukcha*
half	*koos*·kahn	*kuskan*
to halt (oneself)	*sah*·yai	*sayay*
to halt (someone else)	*sah·yah*·chee	*sayachiy*
handbag	*ch'oos*·pah	*ch'uspa*
handsome	*soo*·mahkh	*sumaq*
hand-woven	*mah·kee*·wahn ah·*wahs*·kah	*makiwan awasqa*
happy	*koo*·see • koo·*sees*·kah	*kusi* • *kusisqa*
hard (difficult)	*sah*·sah	*sasa*
to have	*kai*	*kay*
he	*pai*	*pay*
to heal	*hahm*·pee	*hampiy*
healer	*hahm*·pekh	*hampiq*
health	*k-hah*·lee kai	*qhali kay*
to hear	*oo·yah*·ree	*uyariy*
to heat	*roo*·p-hai	*ruphay*
heaven	*hah·*nahkh *pah*·chah	*hanaq pacha*
heavy	*lyah*·sah	*llasa*
to help	*yah·nah*·pai	*yanapay*

Help me!	
yah·nah·pah·*wai*!	¡Yanapawáy!

herb	*ko*·rah	*qura*
herbalist	*ko·rah*·wahn *kahm*·pekh	*qurawan qampiq*
here	*kai*·pee	*kaypi*

Hey!	
yow!	¡Yaw!

high	*soo*·nee	*suni*
hike/to hike	*poo*·ree	*puriy*
hill	*or·ko*·chah	*urqucha*
to hire	*ahl·kee*·lai	*alkilay*
to hold	*hah*·p'ee	*hap'iy*
hole	*t'o*·ko	*t'uqu*
holiday	*p-hees*·tah	*phista*
home	*wah·see ai*·lyoo	*wasi ayllu*
honest	*soo*·mahkh	*sumaq*
	kow·sai·*nee*·yokh	*kawsayniyuq*
honey	*ah·nyah*·kah	*añaka*
honeycomb	*lah·chee·wah*·nah	*lachiwana*
hope	*soo*·yai	*suyay*

horrible	*mee*·lyai	*millay*
horse	kah·*wah*·lyoo	*kawallu*
to ride a horse	see·*lyah*·kui	*sillakuy*
hospital	*hahm*·pee·nah *wah*·see	*hampina wasi*
hot	*roo*·p·hah	*rupha*
to be hot (person)	*roo*·p·*hah*·ree	*ruphariy*
house	*wah*·see	*wasi*
how	ee·*mai*·nah	*imayna*
how much	*hai*·k'ahn	*hayk'an*
to hug	mah·*k'ah*·lyee	*mak'alliy*
to hug each other	mah·k'ah·lyee·*nah*·kui	*mak'allinakuy*
humankind	*roo*·nah	*runa*
to be hungry	*yahr*·kai	*yarqay*
to hurt	*nah*·nai	*nanay*

I

I	*no*·kah • *nyo*·kah	*nuqa* • *ñuqa*
ice	ch·hoo·*lyoon*·koo	*chhullunku*
if	*see*·choos	*sichus*
ill	on·*kos*·kah	*unqusqa*
to imitate	kah·tee·*chee*·kui	*qatichikuy*
immediately	koo·*nah*·lyahn	*kunallan*
important	chah·*nee*·yokh	*chaniyuq*
in	·pee	*-pi*
in a hurry	ah·poo·*rahs*·kah	*apurasqa*
Inca	*een*·kah	*inka*
(to become) infected	*ch'oo*·pui	*ch'upuy*
(to become) inflamed	*poon*·kee	*punkiy*
to inform	*wee*·lyai	*willay*
injury	*k'ee*·ree	*k'iri*
inside	oo·*k·hoo*·pee	*ukhupi*
instructor	yah·*chah*·chekh	*yachachiq*
intelligent	yah·chai·*nee*·yokh	*yachayniyuq*
to introduce (a person)	rekh·*see*·chee	*riqsichiy*
island	*wah*·t'ah	*wat'a*
itch (sensation)	*sekh*·see	*siqsiy*

J

jar	*oor*·poo	*urpu*
job	lyahn·*k'ah*·nah	*llank'ana*
to join	hookh·*lyah*·kui	*hukllakuy*
joke	*chahn*·sah	*chansa*
to joke	chahn·*sah*·kui	*chansakuy*
joker (comedian)	ah·see·*chee*·kokh	*asichikuq*

K

journey	kah·roo poo·ree	karu puriy
juice	hee·lyee	hilli
to jump	p'ee·tai	p'itay
jungle	yoon·kah	yunka

K

to keep	wah·kai·chai	waqaychay
to keep something for someone else	choo·rah·pui	churapuy
key	p'oo·tee • lyah·wee	p'uti • llawi
to kick	hai·t'ai	hayt'ay
to kill	wah·nyoo·chee	wañuchiy
kind (nice)	k·hoo·yah·kokh	khuyakuq
kind (type)	reekh·ch'ahkh	rikch'aq
to kiss	moo·ch'ai	much'ay
kitchen	koo·see·nah	kusina
knapsack	k'e·pee	q'ipi
knife	koo·choo·nah	kuchuna
to know (a fact)	yah·chai	yachay
to know (people or places)	rekh·see	riqsiy

L

lake	ko·chah	qucha
land	ahly·pah	allpa
language	ree·mai • see·mee	rimay • simi
large	hah·toon	hatun
last	kai·nah	qayna
late	tai·ree	tayri
to be late	tai·ree·yai	tayriyay
to laugh	ah·see	asiy
lazy	ke·lyah	qilla
leader	kah·mah·chekh	kamachiq
to lead	poo·sai	pusay
to learn	yah·chai	yachay
leather	kah·rah	qara
to leave (go away)	lyokh·see	lluqsiy
to leave something	sah·kay	saqiy
to be left over (in excess)	poo·chui	puchuy
left (not right)	lyo·k'e	lluq'i
left-handed	lyo·k'en·choo	lluq'inchu
to lend (durable items)	mah·nyai	mañay
to lend (consumables/money)	mah·nui	manuy
to lend a hand	ai·nee	ayniy

K
D
I
C
T
I
O
N
A
R
Y

letter	kel·kah	qilqa
liar	lyoo·lyah	llulla
to lie (be untruthful)	lyoo·lyah·kui	llullakuy
to lie down	see·ree	siriy
life	kow·sai	kawsay
light (in weight)	ch·hah·lyah	chhalla
light (illumination)	k'ahn·chai	k'anchay
to like	moo·nai	munay
like (like this)	hee·nah	hina
liquor	trah·woo	trawu
to listen	oo·yah·ree	uyariy
little (small)	hoo·ch'ui	huch'uy
a little bit	pee·see pee·see·lyah	pisi pisilla
to live	kow·sai	kawsay
to live in	tee·yai	tiyay
lock	kahn·dah·roo·wahn	kandaruwan
	wees·k'ai	wisq'ay
to lock	wees·k'ah·nah	wisq'ana
long (length)	sui·t'oo	suyt'u
to look/look after	k·hah·wai	qhaway
to look for	mahs·k·hai	maskhay
to look like	reekh·ch'ah·kui	rikch'akuy
loose	wah·yah	waya
lost	cheen·kahs·kah	chinkasqa
a lot (quantity)	ahs·k·hah	askha
love/to love (affection)	k·hoo·yai	khuyay
love/to love (want/desire)	moo·nai	munay
love/to love (intense)	wai·lyui	waylluy
to (be in) love	son·ko too·pah·chee	sunqu tupachiy
to (fall in) love	moo·nah·nah·kui	munanakuy
to (fall in) love (intense)	wai·lyoo·nah·kui	wayllunakuy
lover	moo·nahkh • wai·lyokh	munaq • waylluq
luck	sah·mee	sami
lucky	sah·mee·yokh	samiyuq
lunch	ahl·moo·sai	almusay

M

made of	·mahn·tah	-manta
made of stone	roo·mee·mahn·tah	rumi-manta
main road	hah·toon nyahn	hatun ñan
main square	plah·sah	plasa
to make	roo·wai	ruway
man	k·hah·ree	qhari
mankind	roo·nah	runa
many	ahs·k·hah	askha

map	mah·pah	mapa
market	k-hah·too • plah·sah	qhatu • plasa
marriage	kah·sah·rah·kui	kasarakuy
marvellous	ahn·chah soo·mahkh	ancha sumaq
Mass (Catholic)	mee·sah	misa
match (sport)	pookh·lyai	pukllay
match (to light fires)	foos·poo·roo	phuspuru
to matter	chah·nee·yokh kai	chaniyuq kay

It doesn't matter.
mah·nahn ee·mah·nahn·pahs·choo   *Manan imananpaschu.*

What's the matter?
ee·mah·tahkh soo·see·dee·soon·kee?   *¿Imataq susidisunki?*

mayor	ahl·kahl·dee	alkaldi
medicine	hahm·pee	hampi
medium	tahkh·sah	taksa
to meet	teen·kui	tinkuy
to meet up with	too·pai	tupay
menu	mee·noo	minu
message	wee·lyah·chee·kui	willachikuy
middle (in the)	chow·peen·pee	chawpinpi
milk	lee·chee	lichi
mirror	leer·poo	lirpu
to miss (person)	wah·too·kui	watukuy
mistake (make a)	pahn·tai	pantay
to mix	tahkh·roy	taqruy
money	kol·ke	qulqi
month	kee·lyah	killa
mosquito net	moos·kee·tee·roo	muskitiru
moon	kee·lyah	killa
more	ahs·wahn	aswan
more or less	yah·kah	yaqa
much	ahn·chah	ancha
mud	t'oo·roo	t'uru
music	moo·see·kah	musika
musician	moo·see·koo	musiku

N

name	soo·tee	suti
to name	soo·tee·chai	sutichay
narrow	k'eekh·lyoo	k'ikllu
nation	lyahkh·tah	llaqta
nature	kow·sai pah·chah	kawsay pacha
near	sees·pah • kai·lyah	sispa • qaylla

neck	koon·kah	kunka
necklace	wahl·kah	walqa
to need	moo·nai	munay
needle (sewing)	ah·woo·hah	awuha
needle (large)	yow·ree	yawri
neighbour	wah·see·mah·see	wasi-masi
never	mah·nah hai·k'ahkh·pahs	mana hayk'aqpas
new	moo·sokh	musuq
news	wee·lyai·koo·nah	willaykuna
next (following)	hah·mokh • kah·tekh	hamuq • qatiq
next to	wahkh·tahn·pee	waqtanpi
nice	ah·lyeen	allin
nickname	k-hoo·yai soo·tee	khuyay suti
night	too·tah • ch'ee·see	tuta • ch'isi
noise	rokh·yah	ruqya
none	mah·nah	mana
	ch'oo·lyah·lyah·pahs • mah·nah mai·ken	ch'ullallapas • mana mayqin
north	wee·chai	wichay
nothing	mah·nahn ee·mah·pahs	manan imapas
not yet	mah·nah·rahkh	manaraq
now	koo·nahn	kunan

O

ocean	ko·chah·mah·mah	quchamama
of (poss)	·kh • ·pah	-q • -pa
of course	ree·kee	riki
often	nyah·tahkh·nyah·tahkh	ñataq-ñataq
old (age)	mah·choo	machu
old (worn out)	t-han·tah	thanta
on	·pee	-pi

It's on the table.
mee·sah·pee kah·shahn.   *Misa-pi kashan.*

one	hokh	huq
onions	see·wee·lyah	siwilla
only	·lyah	-lla
open	kee·chahs·kah	kichasqa
to open	kee·chai	kichay
opinion	hah·moo·t'ai	hamut'ay
or	ee·chah • oo·tahkh	icha • utaq
to organise	ah·lyee·chai	allichay
original	kahkh kee·keen	kaq kikin
other	hokh	huq

Ouch!		
ah·chah·*kow*!		¡Achakáw!

outside	*hah*·wah	*hawa*
over	*hah*·wahn	*hawan*
overcoat	p'ees·*too*·nah	*p'istuna*
to owe (money)	*mah*·noo kai	*manu kay*
owl	*too*·koo	*tuku*
owner	*dui*·nyoo	*duyñu*

P

package	*k'e*·pee	*q'ipi*
pain	*nah*·nai	*nanay*
painkillers	*nah*·nai t-ha·*nee*·chekh	*nanay thanichiq*
to paint	*lyoo*·see	*llusiy*
painter	*lyoo*·sekh	*llusiq*
pants	pahn·*tah*·loon	*pantalun*
paper	*rah*·p'ah • *rah*·p-hee	*rap'a • raphi*
park	pook·*lyah*·nah *pahm*·pah	*pukllana pampa*
party	*fees*·tah	*phista*
to pass (hand to)	*hai*·wai	*hayway*
to pass (on the street)	*pah*·sai	*pasay*
to pass (cross a bridge/river)	*cheem*·pai	*chimpay*
passenger	pah·sah·*hee*·roo	*pasahiru*
past (remote, undefined time)	*oo*·nai • *nyow*·pah	*unay • ñawpa*
path	*nyahn*	*ñan*
patient (adj)	*lyah*·k-hee	*llakhi*
to pay	koy • *pah*·gai	*quy • pagay*
payment	*pah*·goo	*pagu*
peace	*kah*·see *kow*·sai	*qasi kawsay*
peak (of a mountain)	*poon*·tah	*punta*
peas	ahl·*weer*·hahs	*alwirhas*
pen/pencil	kel·*kah*·nah	*qilqana*
people	roo·nah·*koo*·nah	*runakuna*
perhaps	ee·chah·pahs·*chah*	*ichapaschá*
person	*roo*·nah	*runa*
pharmacy	hahm·*pee*·yokh *wah*·see	*hampiyuq wasi*
photo	*foo*·too	*phutu*
photographer	*foo*·too *kor*·kokh	*phutu qurquq*
to pick up (lift)	ho·*kah*·ree	*huqariy*
to pick up (gather, collect)	*pah*·lyai	*pallay*

English	Pronunciation	Quechua
piece	ahkh·no • k'ookh·moo	aqnu • k'ukmu
pill	pahs·tee·lyah	pastilla
pillow	sow·nah	sawna
place	pah·chah	pacha
plane	ah·wee·yoon	awiyun
plant	ko·rah • yoo·rah	qura • yura
to plant (trees)	mahly·kee	mallkiy
to plant (sow)	tahr·pui	tarpuy
to plant (vegetables)	yoo·rai	yuray
plate	p'oo·koo	p'uku
to play (games or sport)	pookh·lyai	pukllay
to play (music)	wah·kah·chee	waqachiy
playing field (sport)	pookh·lyah·nah	pukllana
	pahm·pah	pampa
plenty	ahs·k·hah	askha
pocket	wool·see·koo	wulsiku
poem	hah·rah·wee	harawi
police	wahr·dee·yah	wardiya
pond	ko·chah	qucha
poor/poor person	wahkh·chah	wakcha
possible	ah·tee·nah·lyah	atinalla
pot	mahn·kah	manka
pottery	rahkh·ch'ee	raqch'i
poverty	wahkh·chah kai	wakcha kay
power (ability)	ah·tee	atiy
power (strength)	kahly·pah	kallpa
powerful (rich/influential)	k·hah·pahkh	qhapaq
powerful (dominant)	ah·tee·pahkh	atipaq
to pray	mah·nyah·kui	mañakuy
to prefer	moo·nai	munay
pregnant (humans)	weekh·sah·yokh	wiksayuq
pregnant (animals)	chee·choo	chichu
to prepare	kah·mah·ree	kamariy
present (gift)	ree·k·hoo·chee·kui	rikhuchikuy
present (now)	koo·nahn • kah·nahn	kunan • kanan
pretty	soo·mahkh	sumaq
price (fair price)	chah·neen	chanin
probably	ee·chah·pahs	ichapas
to protect	ah·mah·chai	amachay
to pull	ai·sai	aysay
pure (water)	ch'oo·yah	ch'uya
purse with shoulder strap	ch'oos·pah	ch'uspa
to push	tahn·kai	tanqay
to put	choo·rai	churay

Q

Quechua speakers	*roo*·nah	*runa*
Quechua	roo·nah·*see*·mee	*runasimi*
question	tah·*poo*·nah	*tapuna*
to question	*tah*·pui	*tapuy*
quick	*p-hah*·wahkh • *oot*·k-hahkh	*phawaq* • *utqhaq*
quickly (motion)	p-hah·*wai*·lyah • oos·*k-hai*·lyah	*phawaylla* • *usqhaylla*
quickly (time)	rah·*too*·lyah	*ratulla*
quiet (silence)	ch'een	*ch'in*
quinoa (Andean grain)	*keen*·wah • *kyoo*·nyah	*kinwa* • *kiwña*

R

race (contest)	*p-hah*·wai	*phaway*
radio	rah·*dee*·yoo	*radiyu*
rain	*pah*·rah	*para*
to rain	*pah*·rai	*paray*
raw (uncooked)	*hahn*·koo	*hanku*
to read	*lee*·yee • nyah·*ween*·chai	*liyiy* • *ñawinchay*
ready	kah·mah·*rees*·kah	*kamarisqa*
real (genuine)	*che*·kahkh	*chiqaq*
reason	·*rai*·koo	*-rayku*
to receive	*chahs*·kee	*chaskiy*
recently	*chai*·rahkh	*chayraq*
to recognise	*rekh*·see	*riqsiy*
to refund	koo·tee·*chee*·pui	*kutichipuy*
to refuse	*ah*·mah nee	*ama niy*
region	*soo*·yoo	*suyu*
to regret	nah·nah·*chee*·kui	*nanachikuy*
to reject	*ah*·mah nee	*ama niy*
to relax	*how*·kay	*hawkay*
to remain	*k-he*·pai	*qhipay*
to remember	*yoo*·yai	*yuyay*
remote	kah·roo kah·roo	*karu karu*
to rent	ahl·*kee*·lai	*alkilay*
to repeat	koo·*tee*·pai	*kutipay*
to respect	yoo·*pai*·chai	*yupaychay*
rest/to rest (relax)	*sah*·mai	*samay*
rest (remaining)	*wah*·keen	*wakin*
restaurant	mee·*k-hoo*·nah *wah*·see	*mikhuna wasi*
restroom	hees·*p'ah·koo*·nah	*hisp'akuna*
to return (come back)	koo·*tee*·mui	*kutimuy*
rice	*ah*·roos	*arus*
to ride (a horse)	see·*lyah*·kui	*sillakuy*

ENGLISH – QUECHUA DICTIONARY

right (correct)	chah·neen	chanin
right (not left)	pah·nyah	paña
ring (jewellery)	see·wee	siwi
ripe	po·kos·kah	puqusqa
river	mah·yoo	mayu
road	nyahn	ñan
to rob	soo·wah·kui	suwakuy
rock (stone)	roo·mee	rumi
rope	wahs·k·hah	waskha
round	moo·yoo	muyu
rubbish	k'o·pah	q'upa
rug	kom·pee	qumpi
ruins	nyow·pah lyahkh·tah •	ñawpa llaqta •
	poo·roon lyahkh·tah	purun llaqta
rule	kah·mah·chee	kamachiy
to run	p·hah·wai	phaway

S

sad	lyah·kees·kah	llakisqa
safe	k·hah·lee·lyah	qhalilla
salt	kah·chee	kachi
same	kee·kee	kiki
sand	ah·ko	aqu
to save (a person)	kes·pee·chee	qispichiy
to say	nee	niy
school	yah·chai wah·see	yachay wasi
scissors	koo·choo·nah	kuchuna
sea	ko·chah·mah·mah	quchamama
to search	mahs·k·hai	maskhay
seat	tee·yah·nah	tiyana
to see	k·hah·wai	qhaway
seed	moo·hoo	muhu
to select	ahkh·lyai	akllay
to sell	been·dee	bindiy
to sell at a market/ fair/stand	k·hah·tui	qhatuy
to send a person (on an errand)	kah·chai	kachay
to separate	t'ah·kai • rah·kee	t'aqay • rakiy
to serve food	kah·rai	qaray
to sew	see·rai	siray
shade/shadow	lyahn·t·hoo	llanthu
to shake hands	lyah·mee·yui	llamiyuy
shampoo	chahm·poo	champu
to share one's food/drink	mah·lyee·chee	mallichiy

to shave	*p'ahkh*·lai	*p'aqlay*
shawl	*lyeekh*·lyah	*lliklla*
she	pai	*pay*
shelf	choo·rah·*ree*·nah	*churarina*
shine	*k'ahn*·chai	*k'anchay*
shop	*teen*·dah	*tinda*
short	*tahkh*·sah	*taksa*
to shout	kah·*pah*·ree	*qapariy*
show	k-hah·*wah*·chee	*qhawachiy*
shut	wees·*k'ahs*·kah	*wisq'asqa*
to shut	wees·*k'ai*	*wisq'ay*
sickness/to get sick	*on*·koy	*unquy*
side	*keen*·rai	*kinray*
sign	oo·*nahn*·chah	*unancha*
to sign (a document)	soo·tee sel·*k'oy*	*suti silq'uy*
signature	*sel*·k'o	*silq'u*
silent	ch'een	*ch'in*
silver	*kol*·ke	*qulqi*
similar	*hee*·nah	*hina*
to sing	*tah*·kee	*takiy*
singer	*tah*·kekh	*takiq*
single man	*mah*·nah wahr·*mee*·yokh	*mana warmiyuq*
single woman	*mah*·nah qo·*sah*·yokh	*mana qusayuq*
single (unique)	*ch'oo*·lyah	*ch'ulla*
to sit	*tee*·yai	*tiyay*
size/to size	*sah*·yai	*sayay*
sky	*hah*·nahkh *pah*·chah	*hanaq pacha*
sky blue	*t'okh*·rah *ahn*·kahs	*t'uqra anqas*
to sleep	poo·nyui	*puñuy*
sleepy	poo·nyui *ai*·sai	*puñuy aysay*
to slide	soo·chui	*suchuy*
slowly	ah·lyee·lyah·*mahn*·tah	*allillamanta*
small	hoo·ch'ui	*huch'uy*
to smell	*moos*·k-hee	*muskhiy*
to smile	ah·see·*ree*·kui	*asirikuy*
smoke	*q'oos*·nyee	*q'usñi*
to smoke (a cigarette)	*pee*·tai	*pitay*
smooth	syookh	*siwk*
to sneeze	*ah*·ch-hee	*achhiy*
snow/to snow	*ree*·t'ee	*rit'i*
so	chai hee·*nah*·kah •	*chay hinaqa* •
	kai·*nah*·tah	*kaynata*
soap	*hah*·woon	*hawun*
soft	*lyahm*·p'oo	*llamp'u*
solid	*ch'ee*·lah • *choo*·choo	*ch'ila* • *chuchu*
some (animate object)	wah·keen·koo·*nah*·lyah	*wakinkunalla*

some (inanimate object)	wah·kee·wah·kee·lyan	wakiwakillan
someone	pee·pahs	pipas
something	ee·mah·pees •	imapis • imapas
	ee·mah·pahs	
sometimes	mai·nee·lyahn·pee	maynillanpi
song (sad)	tah·kee • hah·rah·wee	taki • harawi
soon	koo·nah·lyan	kunallan

Sorry.
dees·peen·sah·yoo·wai   Dispinsayuway.

sound	sui·nai	suynay
Spanish	kahs·tee·lyah·noo	kastillanu
to speak	ree·mai	rimay
speedy	oos·k-hakh	usqhaq
spindle (for spinning)	poos·kah	puska
spring (water)	pookh·yoo	pukyu
square (shape)	tah·wah k'oo·choo·yokh	tawa k'uchuyuq
square (town)	plah·sah	plasa
stairs	pah·tah pah·tah	pata pata
to stand	sah·yai	sayay
stars	koy·lyoor • ch'ahs·kah	quyllur • ch'aska
to start	kah·lyah·ree	qallariy
to stay (remain)	k-he·pai	qhipay
to steal	soo·wai	suway
steam	wahkh·see	waksi
steep	sah·yahkh	sayaq
to step	t-haht·kee	thatkiy
step on	sah·rui	saruy
stone	roo·mee	rumi
to stop (oneself)	sah·yai	sayay
to stop (someone else)	sah·yah·chee	sayachiy
storm	lyokh·lyahh pah·rah	lluqlla para
story	wee·lyah·kui	willakuy
straight	syook	siwk
stranger	mah·nah rek·sees·kah	mana riqsisqa
stream	mah·yoo·chah •	mayucha •
	oo·noo hai·kokh	unu haykuq
street	nyahn • kah·lyee	ñan • kalli
strength	kahly·pah	kallpa
string	k'ai·too	q'aytu
strong (solid)	choo·choo	chuchu
strong (durable)	kah·kah	qaqa
strong (person)	seen·chee	sinchi
student	yah·chai moo·nahkh	yachay munaq

stupid	mah·nah ah·lyeen yoo·yai·nee·yokh	mana allin yuyayniyuq
to succeed	ah·lyeen·wahn lyokh·see	allinwan lluqsiy
to suffer	nyah·kai	ñakay
sugar	mees·k'ee • ah·soo·kahr	misk'i • asukar
suitcase	mah·lee·tah	malita
sunlight	roo·p·hai	ruphay
sunrise	een·tee lyee·pee·pee·mui • lyokh·see·mui	inti llipipimuy • lluqsimuy
sunset	ch'ee·see·yai·pui • een·tee·yai·kui	ch'isiyapuy • intiyakuy
to sweep	pee·chai	pichay
sweet	mees·k'ee	misk'i
to swim	wai·t'ai	wayt'ay

table	wahm·pahr	wampar
to take	ah·pai	apay
to take (on your back)	k'e·pee	q'ipiy
talk	ree·mai	rimay
tall	hah·toon	hatun
tambourine	teen·yah	tinya
to taste	mah·lyee	malliy
tasty	soo·mahkh • mees·k'ee	sumaq • misk'i
teacher	yah·chah·chekh • hah·mow·t'ah	yachachiq • hamawt'a
tear	we·ke	wiqi
teeth	kee·roo	kiru
to tell	nee • wee·lyai	niy • willay
temperature (fever)	roo·p·hai on·koy	ruphay unquy
temple	mahn·ko/yoo·pai·chai wah·see	manqu/yupaychay wasi
terrible	mah·nah ah·lyeen	mana allin
to thank	ah·nyai·chai • sool·pai nee	añaychay • sulpáy niy

Thank you.
ah·nyai·chai·kee • sool·pai   Añaychayki. • Sulpáy.

that	chai • ahn·chai	chay • anchay
that over there	chah·hai • hah·kai	chahay • haqay
them	pai·koo·nah	paykuna
then (at that time)	chai pah·chah	chay pacha
there	chai·pee	chaypi
they	pai·koo·nah	paykuna

T

thief	*soo·wah*	*suwa*
thin (skinny)	*too·lyoo*	*tullu*
to think	*yoo·yai*	*yuyay*
thirst	*ch'ah·kee*	*ch'akiy*
thirsty	*ch'ah·kees·kah*	*ch'akisqa*
this	*kai*	*kay*
thought	*yoo·yai*	*yuyay*
to tie	*wah·tai*	*watay*
tight	*mah·t'ee*	*mat'i*
time	*pah·chah*	*pacha*
tin (of food)	*lah·tah*	*lata*
tin opener	*lah·tah kee·chah·nah*	*lata kichana*
tired	*sai·k'oos·kah*	*sayk'usqa*
today	*koo·nahn p'oon·chai*	*kunan p'unchay*
together	*koos·kah*	*kuska*
toilet	*hees·p'ah·koo·nah*	*hisp'akuna*
tomorrow	*pah·kah·reen*	*paqarin*
too	*·pees • ·pahs*	*-pis • -pas*

> Me too.
> no·*kah*·pees•
> nyo·*kah*·pahs.
>
> *Nuqa-pis.•*
> *Ñuqa-pas.*

too much	*chee·kah chee·kah*	*chika chika*
torch	*k'ahn·chah·nah*	*k'anchana*
to touch	*lyah·mee*	*llamiy*
tourist	*too·rees·tah*	*turista*
towards/to	*·mahn • ·tah*	*-man • -ta*
towel	*too·wah·lyah*	*tuwalla*
town	*lyahkh·tah*	*llaqta*
track (path)	*nyahn*	*ñan*
to translate	*t'eekh·rai*	*t'ikray*
trash	*k'o·pah*	*q'upa*
to travel	*ch'oo·sai • poo·ree*	*ch'usay • puriy*
traveller	*poo·rekh*	*puriq*
tree	*mahly·kee*	*mallki*
to trek	*kah·roo poo·ree*	*karu puriy*
truck	*kah·mee·yoon*	*kamiyun*
true	*che·kahkh*	*chiqaq*

> It's true!
> che·*kahkh*·mee!
>
> *¡Chiqaqmi!*

to trust	*koon·p-hee·yai*	*kunphiyay*
truth	*che·kahkh*	*chiqaq*

**D
I
C
T
I
O
N
A
R
Y**

to turn	moo·*yoo*·ree	*muyuriy*

> Turn left.
> lyo·*k'e*·mahn moo·*yoo*·ree   *Lluq'iman muyuriy.*
>
> Turn right.
> pah·*nyah*·mahn moo·*yoo*·ree   *Pañaman muyuriy.*

twice	*ees*·kai koo·*tee*	*iskay kuti*

U

under	*pah*·chahn	*pachan*
to understand	een·*teen*·dee	*intindiy*
universe	tekh·see·*moo*·yoo	*tiqsimuyu*
until	·*kah*·mah	*-kama*
up	hah·nahkh	*hanaq*
uphill	*wee*·chai	*wichay*
to be upset	p-hee·*nyah*·kui	*phiñakuy*
urgent	oos·*k-hai*·pahkh	*usqhaypaq*
useful	*ah*·lyeen	*allin*

V

vacation	*sah*·mai *pah*·chah	*samay pacha*
valley	*k-hes*·wah • *wai*·k'o	*qhiswa* • *wayq'u*
valuable	chah·*nee*·yokh	*chaniyuq*
value	*chah*·neen	*chanin*
vegetarian	*mah*·nah ai·chah	*mana aycha*
	mee·kokh	*mikuq*
very	*ahn*·chah	*ancha*
village	*lyahkh*·tah	*llaqta*
to visit	wah·*too*·kui	*watukuy*

W

to wait	*soo*·yai	*suyay*
to walk	*poo*·ree	*puriy*
wall	*per*·kah	*pirqa*
to want	*moo*·nai	*munay*
warm	*k'o*·nyee	*q'uñi*
to warm up	*k'o*·nyee·kui	*q'uñikuy*
to warn	yoo·*yahm*·pai	*yuyampay*
to wash (clothes/hair)	*t'ahkh*·sai	*t'aqsay*
to wash (general, except clothes/hair)	*mahkh*·ch-hee	*maqchhiy*
to wash oneself (bathe)	ahr·*mah*·kui	*armakuy*

washing powder	dee·teer·*heen*·tee	*ditirhinti*
watch	k·*hah*·wai	*qhaway*
to watch	ree·looh	*riluh*
water	oo·noo • *yah*·koo	*unu • yaku*
waterfall	p·hahkh·chah	*phaqcha*
way (path)	nyahn	*ñan*
we (exclusive)	no·*kai*·koo	*nuqayku*
we (inclusive)	no·*kahn*·chees	*nuqanchis*
weak	*kahly*·pah wah·nyui	*kallpa wañuy*
to wear (clothes)	p'ah·chah·*lyee*·kui	*p'achallikuy*
to weave	ah·wai	*away*
wedding	kah·sah·*rah*·kui	*kasarakuy*
week	see·*mah*·nah	*simana*
to weigh	ai·sai	*aysay*
weight	*lyah*·sah	*llasa*
well	ah·lyeen	*allin*
west	*een*·tee cheen·*kai*·kui	*inti chinkaykuy*
wet	ho·k'o	*huq'u*

What?	
ee·*mahn*?	¿Iman?
What! (response to being called)	
hai!/ee·mah!	¡Hay!/¡Ima!
When?	
hai·k'·ahkh?	¿Hayk'aq?
Where?	
mai·peen?	¿Maypin?
From where?	
mai·*mahn*·tahn?	¿Maymantan?
To where?	
mai·*tah*·tahkh?	¿Maytataq?
Which?	
mai·keen?	¿Mayqin?
Who?	
peen? (sg)/pee·*koo*·nahn? (pl)	¿Pin?/¿Pikunan?
Who is it?	
peen?	¿Pin?
Whose?	
pekh·pah?	¿Piqpa?
Why?	
ee·mah·*nahkh*·teen?	¿Imanaqtin?

window	*t'o·*ko • ween·*tah·*nah	*t'uqu* • *wintana*
winter	*chee·*ree mee·*t'*ah	*chiri mit'a*
with	·wahn	*-wan*
with me	no·*kah·*wahn	*nuqa-wan*
woman	*wahr·*mee	*warmi*
wonderful	*ahn·*chah *soo·*mahkh	*ancha sumaq*
wood	*k'oo·*lyoo	*k'ullu*
wool	*meely·*mah	*millma*
word	*ree·*mai • *see·*mee	*rimay* • *simi*
to work	*lyahn·*k'ai	*llank'ay*
world	*pah·*chah •	*pacha* •
	tekh·see·*moo·*yoo	*tiqsimuyu*
worried	lyah·*kees·*kah	*llakisqa*
to worship	yoo·*pai·*chai	*yupaychay*
worth (value)	*chah·*neen	*chanin*
to write	*kel·*kai	*qilqay*
wrong (mistaken)	*pahn·*tah	*panta*

Y

year	*wah·*tah	*wata*
you (sg)	kahn	*qan*
you (pl)	*kahn·*koo·nah	*qankuna*

Z

| zero | *ch'oo·*sahkh | *ch'usaq* |

A

achhiy	*ah·ch·hee*	to sneeze
aha	*ah·hah*	*chicha* (maize beer)
ahinaqa	*ah·hee·nah·kah*	so
akllay	*ahk·lyai*	to choose
aksidinti	*ahkh·see·deen·tee*	accident
akupana	*ah·koo·pah·nah*	sunset
alkaldi	*ahl·kahl·dee*	mayor
alkilay	*ahl·kee·lai*	to hire • to rent
almusay	*ahl·moo·sai*	to have lunch
allillamanta	*ah·lyee·lyah·mahn·tah*	slowly
allin	*ah·lyeen*	good • useful • well
allpa	*ahly·pah*	land • earth (soil)
ama niy	*ah·mah nee*	to refuse • to reject
amachay	*ah·mah·chai*	to protect
amisqa	*ah·mes·kah*	bored • boring
ancha	*ahn·chah*	much • very
apamuy	*ah·pah·mui*	to bring
apay	*ah·pai*	to take
apu	*ah·poo*	rich
apurasqa	*ah·poo·rahs·kah*	in a hurry
aqnu	*ahkh·no*	piece
aqu	*ah·ko*	sand
armakuy	*ahr·mah·kui*	to bathe • to wash oneself
arpha	*ahr·p·hah*	blind (adj)
as aslla	*ahs ahs·lyah*	a little bit
asirikuy	*ah·see·ree·kui*	to smile
asiti	*ah·see·tee*	oil (cooking)
asiy	*ah·see*	to laugh
askamalla	*ahs·kah·mah·lyah*	quickly • fast (time)
askha	*ahs·k·hah*	many • a lot of
asnay	*ahs·nai*	to smell
asukar	*ah·soo·kahr*	sugar
aswan	*ahs·wahn*	more
aswan allin	*ahs·wahn ah·lyeen*	better
aswan hatun	*ahs·wahn hah·toon*	bigger
atinalla	*ah·tee·nah·lyah*	possible
atipaq	*ah·tee·pahkh*	powerful
atipay	*ah·tee·pai*	to put up with
atiy	*ah·tee*	to be able • power • strength
away	*ah·wai*	to weave
awiyun	*ah·wee·yoon*	aeroplane
awtu	*ow·too*	car
awuha	*ah·woo·hah*	needle (sewing)
aya p'ampana	*ah·yah p'ahm·pah·nah*	cemetery
aya sankha	*ah·yah sahn·k·hah*	grave • tomb
aycha kurku	*ai·chah koor·koo*	body

ayllu	ai·lyoo	community • family
aynly	ai·nee	to help out
ayqi	ai·ke	to exit • to leave
aysay	ai·sai	to pull • to stretch

B

| bañu | bah·nyoo | bathroom • toilet |
| bindiy | been·dee | to sell |

CH

chahay	chah·hai	that over there
chaka	chah·kah	bridge • thigh
chakra	chahkh·rah	farm • field (cultivated) • earth (soil)
chanin	chah·neen	fair price • value • worth • right • correct • true
chaniyuq	chah·nee·yokh	important • valuable
chaniyuq kay	chah·nee·yokh kai	to matter (be important)
chansa	chahn·sah	joke
chaskiy	chahs·kee	to receive
chawpinpi	chow·peen·pee	in the middle
chay	chai	that
chay hinaqa	chai hee·nah·kah	so
chay pacha	chai pah·chah	then • at that time
chayasqa	chah·yahs·kah	done (of food)
chayay	chai·yai	to arrive
chayllaña	chai·lyah·nyah	enough
chaymanta	chai·mahn·tah	besides (furthermore)
chaymantaqa	chai·mahn·tah·kah	afterwards
chaypachamanta	chai·pah·chah·mahn·tah	since then
chaypas	chai·pahs	although
chaypi	chai·pee	there
chayraq	chai·rahkh	recently
chimpapi	cheem·pah·pee	across (from)
chimpay	cheem·pai	to pass • to cross over
chinkasqa	cheen·kahs·kah	lost • hidden
chipchiy	cheep·chee	to shine (sun) • to illuminate
chiqanta	che·kahn·tah	straight
chiqaq	che·kahkh	truth • real • genuine
chiskasqa puriy	chees·kahs·kah poo·ree	to be lost
chiyay	chee·yai	to arrive
chuchu	choo·choo	solid • strong
chupi	choo·pee	soup
churanakuy	choo·rah·nah·kui	to argue
churapuy	choo·rah·pui	to keep something for someone else
churarina	choo·rah·ree·nah	shelf

churay	choo·rai	to put • to inject
chusi	choo·see	blanket
chuyk'ucha	chui·k'oo·chah	cup

CHH

chhalay	ch-hah·lai	to barter • to exchange
chhalla	ch-hah·lyah	light (in weight)
chhika	ch-hee·kah	plenty
chhika chhika	ch-hee·kah ch-hee·kah	too much • too many
chhulli	ch-hoo·lyee	influenza
chhullunku	ch-hoo·lyoon·koo	ice
chhuqay	ch-ho·kai	to push

CH'

ch'aka	ch'ah·kah	sore throat • hoarse
ch'aki	ch'ah·kee	dry
ch'akisqa	ch'ah·kees·kah	thirsty
ch'akiy	ch'ah·kee	to dry • to be thirsty • thirst
ch'aska	ch'ahs·kah	stars
ch'ikay	ch'ee·kai	sting (of bee/wasp)
ch'in	ch'een	quiet (silence) • silent
ch'iqmiy	ch'ekh·mee	to bother
ch'isiyay	ch'ee·see·yai	to get dark
ch'ulla	ch'oo·lyah	single (unique)
ch'unku	ch'oon·koo	crowd • group
ch'upuy	ch'oo·pui	to become infected
ch'usaq	ch'oo·sahkh	space • zero • empty
ch'usay	ch'oo·sai	to travel
ch'uspa	ch'oos·pah	small bag • handbag
ch'ustikuy	ch'oos·tee·kui	to undress
ch'uya	ch'oo·yah	clean • pure (of water)

D

| Diyus | dee·yoos | God |
| duktur | dookh·toor | doctor |

H

hamawt'a	hah·mow·t'ah	teacher • professor • community leader • wise
hampi	hahm·pee	drug • medicine
hampina wasi	hahm·pee·nah wah·see	hospital
hampiq	hahm·pekh	healer
hampiy	hahm·pee	to heal • to cure
hampiyuq wasi	hahm·pee·yokh wah·see	drugstore • pharmacy

hamuq	hah·mokh	next (following)
hamuy	hah·mui	to come
hanaq	hah·nahkh	up • above
hanaq pacha	hah·nahkh pah·chah	heaven • sky
hanku	hahn·koo	raw (uncooked)
hanq'ara	hahn·k'ah·rah	dish
hap'iy	hah·p'ee	to hold
haqay	hah·kai	that over there
harawi	hah·rah·wee	poem • song
hark'apay	hahr·k'ah·pai	to protect
hark'ay	hahr·k'ai	to prevent
hasp'ikuy	hahs·p'ee·kui	itch • to scratch
hatun	hah·toon	big • high • large • tall
hawa	hah·wah	outside
hawa runa	hah·wah roo·nah	foreigner
hawanpi	hah·wahn·pee	above
hawan	hah·wahn	over
hawapi	hah·wah·pee	outside
hawkay	how·kai	to relax
hayk'an	hai·k'ahn	how much
hayk'aq	hai·k'ahkh	when
haykuna	hai·koo·nah	gate
haykuy	hai·kui	to enter
hayway	hai·wai	to pass (hand to)
hina	hee·nah	similar • like this/that
hina kaqlla	hee·nah kahkh·lyah	permanent
hinaspa	hee·nahs·pah	besides (furthermore) • thus
hinastin	hee·nahs·teen	everywhere
hisp'akuna	hees·p'ah·koo·nah	toilet • restroom
hisp'akuy	hees·p'ah·kui	to urinate
hucha	hoo·chah	fault • sin
huchallikuy	hoo·chah·lyee·kui	to sin
huch'uy	hoo·ch'ui	small • little
huk'i	hoo·k'ee	corner (inside)
huklla	hookh·lyah	together
hukllakuy	hookh·lyah·kui	to join
hukllay	hookh·lyai	to mix
hunt'a	hoon·t'ah	full (complete)
hunt'asqa	hoon·t'ahs·kah	exact • exactly
huñiy	hoo·nyee	to allow • to permit
hup'a	hoo·p'ah	deaf
huq	hokh	one • another • other
huq ratuña	hokh rah·too·nyah	ago
huqariy	ho·kah·ree	to pick up (lift)
huqmanta	hokh·mahn·tah	again
huqnirayay	hokh·nee·rah·yai	to change (into something) • to become
huq'u	ho·k'o	damp • wet
hurquy	hor·koy	to take

I

icha	*ee·chah*	or
ichapas	*ee·chah·pahs*	probably
ichapaschá	*ee·chah·pahs·chah*	perhaps
imallapas	*ee·mah·lyah·pahs*	anything • something
iman	*ee·mahn*	what
imanaqtin	*ee·mah·nahkh·teen*	why
imayna	*ee·mai·nah*	how
iniy/iñiy	*ee·nee/ee·nyee*	to believe (religious)
inka	*een·kah*	Inca
inlis	*een·lees*	English
inlisa	*een·lee·sah*	church
intindiy	*een·teen·dee*	to understand
isanka	*ee·sahn·kah*	basket
iskay kuti	*ees·kai koo·tee*	twice
iskaynin	*ees·kai·neen*	both

K

kachay	*kah·chai*	to send (on an errand)
kalli	*kah·lyee*	street
kallpa	*kahly·pah*	strength
kallpa wañuy	*kahly·pah wah·nyui*	weak
-kama	*·kah·mah*	until
kamachiy	*kah·mah·chee*	to order • to rule
kamarikuy	*kah·mah·ree·kui*	to decide
kamarisqa	*kah·mah·rees·kah*	ready
kamariy	*kah·mah·ree*	to prepare
kambiyay	*kahm·bee·yai*	to change
kamisa	*kah·mee·sah*	shirt
kanallan	*kah·nah·lyahn*	immediately • very soon
kanasta	*kah·nahs·tah*	basket
kandaruwan wisq'ay	*kahn·dah·roo·wahn wees·k'ai*	to lock
kaniy	*kah·nee*	bite (of any creature)
kaq kikin	*kahkh kee·keen*	original
karu	*kah·roo*	far
karu llaqta	*kah·roo lyahkh·tah*	abroad
karu llaqta runa	*kah·roo lyahkh·tah roo·nah*	foreigner
karu puriy	*kah·roo poo·ree*	journey • trek
karru	*kah·rroo*	car • truck
kasarakuqmasi	*kah·sah·rah·kokh·mah·see*	fiancé • fiancée
kasarakuy	*kah·sah·rah·kui*	to marry • marriage • wedding
kastillanu	*kahs·tee·lyah·noo*	Spanish
katuliku	*kah·too·lee·koo*	Catholic

kawra	kow·rah	goat
kawsay pacha	kow·sai *pah*·chah	nature
kay	kai	to exist • to be • to have • this
kaynata	kai·*nah*·tah	so
kaypi	kai·pee	here
kichasqa	kee·*chahs*·kah	open
kichay	kee·chai	to open
kiki	kee·kee	same
killa	kee·lyah	month • moon
kinray	keen·rai	side
kinwa	keen·wah	quinoa (Andean grain)
kirpu	keer·poo	body
kuchuna	koo·*choo*·nah	knife • scissors
kuchuy	koo·chui	to cut
kunallan	koo·*nah*·lyan	immediately • very soon
kunan	koo·nahn	now • present (now)
kunan pacha	koo·nahn *pah*·chah	right now
kunphiyay	koon·*p-hee*·yai	to trust
kuntra	koon·trah	against
kura	koo·rah	priest
kurku	koor·koo	body
kusa	koo·sah	nice • right (interjection)
kusa kusa	koo·sah koo·sah	great (quality) • marvellous • wonderful
kusi	koo·see	happy
kusikuy	koo·*see*·kui	to have fun
kusisqa	koo·*sees*·kah	happy
kuska	koos·kah	side by side • together
kuskachakuy	koos·kah·*chah*·kui	to join
kutichipuy	koo·tee·*chee*·pui	to refund • compensation
kutichiy	koo·tee·chee	to answer
kutimuy	koo·tee·mui	to return (come back)
kutipay	koo·tee·pai	to repeat
kutuna	koo·*too*·nah	jacket (of a woman)
kwistay	kwees·tai	to cost

KH

khachuy	k-hah·chui	to bite (dog) • to bite off
kharka	k-hahr·kah	dirty
khumpa	k-hoom·pah	friend
khutu	k-hoo·too	frozen (solid)
khuyakuq	k-hoo·*yah*·kokh	kind (nice)
khuyay	k-hoo·yai	love/to love
khuyay suti	k-hoo·yai soo·tee	nickname

K'

k'akra	k'ahk·rah	ceramic
k'allma	k'ahly·mah	branch
k'anay	k'ah·nai	to burn • to set fire to
k'anchay	k'ahn·chai	to shine (sun) • to illuminate • light
k'apak	k'ah·pahkh	exact • exactly
k'aphra	k'ah·p-hrah	ceramic
k'awchi	k'ow·chee	jar
k'ikllu	k'eek·lyoo	narrow
k'iri	k'ee·ree	injury • wound
k'irikuy	k'ee·ree·kui	to wound
k'uchu	k'oo·choo	corner (outside)
k'ukmu	k'ookh·moo	piece
k'uku	k'oo·koo	short (in distance)
k'utuy	k'oo·tui	bite (insect) • to bite (hard things)

L

laranha	lah·rahn·hah	orange (fruit)
lata	lah·tah	can (of food)
lata kichana	lah·tah kee·chah·nah	can opener
lawa	lah·wah	soup
lintirna	leen·teer·nah	torch • flashlight
lirpu	leer·poo	mirror
liyiy	lee·yee	to read
lus	loos	electric light
luylu	lui·loo	clean

LL

-lla	·lyah	only
llakhi	lyah·k-hee	patient
llakisqa	lyah·kees·kah	sad • worried
llakllay	lyahkh·lyai	to sense • to feel
llamiy	lyah·mee	to feel (touch)
llamiyuy	lyah·mee·yui	to shake hands
llamp'u	lyahm·p'oo	soft
llank'ana	lyahn·k'ah·nah	job
llanthu	lyahn·t-hoo	shade • shadow
llapa	lyah·pah	everything • every • all
llapan	lyah·pahn	everyone
llapanku	lyah·pahn·koo	everyone
llaqta	lyahkh·tah	city • community • country • nation • town • village

llasa	*lyah*·sah	heavy • weight
llimpi	*lyeem*·pee	colour
lliw	*lyoo*	every • all • everything
lliwninku	*lyoo*·neen·koo	everyone
llulla	*lyoo*·lyah	liar
llullakuy	*lyoo*·lyah·kui	to lie (be untruthful)
llumpaq	*lyoom*·pahkh	pure • innocent
llumpay sumaq	*lyoom*·pai soo·mahkh	wonderful
llunch'iq	*lyoon*·ch'ekh	painter
lluq'i	*lyo*·k'e	left (not right)
lluq'inchu	*lyo*·k'en·choo	left-handed
lluqsiy	*lyokh*·see	to depart • to exit • to go away
llusiy	*lyoo*·see	to colour • to paint

machasqa/machaq	mah·*chahs*·kah/ mah·chahkh	drunk
machu	*mah*·choo	old (age)
machay	*mah*·chai	to get drunk
mahanakuy	mah·kah·*nah*·kui	fight • to fight
makiwan awasqa	mah·*kee*·wahn ah·*wahs*·kah	hand-woven
mak'allinakuy	mah·k'ah·lyee·*nah*·kui	to hug each other
mak'alliy	mah·*k'ah*·lyee	to hug
mak'as	*mah*·k'ahs	jar
malita	mah·*lee*·tah	luggage • suitcase
malqu	*mahl*·ko	chick
malliy	*mah*·lyee	to taste
malliyachiy	mah·lyee·*yah*·chee	to share one's food • to drink with someone
mallki mallki	*mahly*·kee *mahly*·kee	forest
mallkiy	*mahly*·kee	to plant
mama	*mah*·mah	mother • Mrs • Madam
-man	·mahn	towards • to
mana allin	*mah*·nah ah·lyeen	bad •
mana allin yuyayniyuq	*mah*·nah ah·lyeen yoo·yai·*nee*·yokh	stupid
mana mayqin	*mah*·nah *mai*·ken	none
mana qasiq	*mah*·nah kah·sekh	busy
mana qusayuq	*mah*·nah qo·*sah*·yokh	single woman
mana riqsisqa	*mah*·nah rek·sees·kah	stranger
mana warmiyuq	*mah*·nah wahr·mee·yokh	single man
manan imapas	*mah*·nahn ee·*mah*·pahs	nothing

Quechua	Pronunciation	English
manan niy	mah·nahn nee	to deny
manaraq	mah·*nah*·rahk	not yet
manchakuy	mahn·*chah*·kui	to be afraid • fear
manchay	*mahn*·chai	danger
manka	*mahn*·kah	pan • pot
-manta	:*mahn*·tah	from • made of
manu kay	*mah*·noo kai	to owe (money)
manuy	mah·nui	to lend (consumables/money)
mañakuy	mah·*nyah*·kui	to ask (for something) • to borrow • to pray
mañay	mah·nyai	to lend (durable items)
map'a	mah·p'ah	awful
maqanakuy	mah·kah·*nah*·kui	to argue
maqchhiy	*mahkh*·ch-hee	to wash (general, not clothes/hair)
masi	*mah*·see	companion • member (club)
maskhay	*mahs*·k-hai	to look for • to search
mat'i	*mah*·t'ee	tight
mat'isqa	mah·*t'ees*·kah	tight
maypin	*mai*·peen	where
maymantan	mai·*mahn*·tahn	from where
maytataq	mai·*tah*·tahkh	to where
mayqin	*mai*·keen	which
michiy	*mee*·chee	to pasture
mihuy	*mee*·hui	to eat • food • lunch
mikhuna wasi	mee·k·*hoo*·nah *wah*·see	restaurant
mik'i	*mee*·k'ee	slightly damp
millay	*mee*·lyai	ugly
millay millay	*mee*·lyai *mee*·lyai	horrible (appearance)
misa	*mee*·sah	Mass (Catholic worship service)
misk'i	*mees*·k'ee	sweet • delicious • tasty • honey • sugar
much'ay	*moo*·ch'ai	to kiss • to worship
muhu	*moo*·hoo	seed
munakuq	moo·*nah*·kokh	kind (nice)
munanakuy	moo·nah·*nah*·kui	to love (fall in)
munay	*moo*·nai	love • to love • to want • to desire • to prefer
munaq	*moo*·nahkh	lover
muskhiy	*moos*·k-hee	to smell
musqhuy	*mos*·k-hoy	dream • to dream
musuq	*moo*·sokh	new
muya	*moo*·yah	garden (fruit)
muyu	*moo*·yoo	round
muyuriy	moo·*yoo*·ree	to turn

D
I
C
T
I
O
N
A
R
Y

N

nanachikuy	nah·nah·chee·kui	to regret • to resent
nanay	nah·nai	to hurt • physical pain
nanay thanichiq	nah·nai t-ha·nee·chekh	painkillers
naqha	nah·k-hah	ago
niy	nee	to say • to tell

Ñ

-ña	·nyah	already
ñakay	nyah·kai	to suffer
ñakariy	nyah·kah·ree	to suffer
ñan	nyahn	path • road • way
ñaña	nyah·nyah	friend (female friend to female) • sister (of woman)
ñanta riqsichiq	nyahn·tah rekh·see·chekh	guide (person)
ñapu	nyah·poo	ripe
ñaqch'a	nyahkh·ch'ah	comb
ñaqha	nyah·k-hah	ago
ñawinchay	nyah·ween·chai	to read
ñawpa	nyow·pah	past • ancient
ñawpa llaqta	nyow·pah lyahkh·tah	ruins
ñawpaq	nyow·pahkh	ahead • past • ancient
ñawpaq kaq	nyow·pahkh kahkh	first
ñawpaqta	nyow·pahkh·tah	before (time)
ñawsa	nyow·sah	blind (adj)
ñiqin	nyeh·ken	first

P

-pa	·pah	of
pacha	pah·chah	world • universe • space • time
pacha kuyuy	pah·chah koo·yui	earthquake
pacha phuyu	pah·chah p-hoo·yoo	fog
pachan	pah·chahn	under
pagu	pah·goo	payment
pallay	pah·lyai	to pick up • to collect
pampa	pahm·pah	countryside • flat place • floor • plain
pampachay	pahm·pah·chai	to forgive
pana/pani	pah·nah/pah·nee	friend (female friend to male) • sister (of man)
panta	pahn·tah	wrong • mistaken
pantalun	pahn·tah·loon	trousers
pantay	pahn·tai	to make a mistake

QUECHUA – ENGLISH DICTIONARY

paña	pah·nyah	right (not left)
paqta	pahkh·tah	perhaps
para	pah·rah	rain
pasahiru	pah·sah·hee·roo	passenger
pasaq kutilla	pah·sahkh koo·tee·lyah	constantly • always
pasay	pah·sai	to pass (on the street)
pasayuy	pah·sah·yui	to enter
pastilla	pahs·tee·lyah	pill
pata	pah·tah	over • on
patapi	pah·tah·pee	above
phukuna waqra	p-hoo·koo·nah wahkh·rah	Andean horn
pin	peen	who
-pi	·pee	on • in • at
pichay	pee·chai	to clean • to sweep
pikaq	pee·kahkh	scorpion
piluta	pee·loo·tah	ball
pipas	pee·pahs	someone
piqpa	pekh·pah	whose
pirqa	per·kah	wall
pirqachay	per·kah·chai	to build
-pis	·pees	also • too • and
pisi	pee·see	few • little • scarce
pisi pisilla	pee·see pee·see·lyah	a little bit
pitay	pee·tai	to smoke (a cigarette)
plasa	plah·sah	plaza
prisisaqpaq	pree·see·sahkh·pahkh	urgent
puchuy	poo·chui	be left over (excess)
pukara	poo·kah·rah	fort • fortress
pukllana pampa	pook·lyah·nah pahm·pah	park • playing field
pukllapayay	pook·lyah·pah·yai	to make fun of
pukllay	pookh·lyai	to play (game/sport) • game • match (sport)
pukyu	pook·yoo	spring (water)
punta	poon·tah	peak (mountain)
puñuna	poo·nyoo·nah	bed
puñuy	poo·nyui	to sleep
puñuy aysay	poo·nyui ai·sai	sleepy
puqusqa	po·kos·kah	ripe
puquy	po·koy	to produce
puriq	poo·rekh	traveller
puriy	poo·ree	to hike • to walk • to travel • trip
purun llaqta	poo·roon lyahkh·tah	ruins
pusamuy	poo·sah·mui	to fetch
pusaq	poo·sahkh	guide (person)
pusay	poo·sai	to lead • to guide
puskay	poos·kai	to spin (thread)

PH

phasil	*fah*·seel	easy
phawaq	p-*hah*·wahkh	quick
phaway	p-*hah*·wai	to fly • to run • race
phawariy	p-hah·*wah*·ree	to run
phawaylla	p-hah·*wai*·lyah	fast (movement) • quickly
phiña	p-*hee*·nyah	angry
phistihay	fees·*tee*·hai	to celebrate
phukuy	p-*hoo*·kui	to play (music)
phuspuru	p-hoos·*poo*·roo	match (to light fires)

P'

p'acha	p'*ah*·chah	dress • clothes
p'achallikuy	p'ah·chah·*lyee*·kui	to wear clothes • to dress oneself
p'akisqa	p'ah·*kees*·kah	broken
p'akiy	p'*ah*·kee	to break
p'alta	p'*ahl*·tah	flat
p'inqasqa	p'en·*kahs*·kah	embarrassed
p'itay	p'*ee*·tai	to jump
p'uchukay	p'oo·*choo*·kai	to finish
p'uku	p'*oo*·koo	dish • plate
p'uti	p'*oo*·tee	key • lock

Q

-q	·kh	of
qallariy	kah·*lyah*·ree	to begin • to start
qanra	*kahn*·rah	dirty
qaparqachay	kah·pahr·*kah*·chai	to scream
qaqa	*kah*·kah	cliff • stone • rock • strong • durable
qara	*kah*·rah	leather • skin
qaray	*kah*·rai	to serve food • to feed
qasa	*kah*·sah	ice
qasay	*kah*·sai	to freeze
qasi kawsay	kah·see *kow*·sai	peace
qata	*kah*·tah	blanket
qatichikuy	kah·tee·*chee*·kui	to copy
qatiq	*kah*·tekh	next • following • descendant
qatiy	*kah*·tee	to follow
qaylla	*kai*·lyah	near
qayna	*kai*·nah	last
qayqa	*kai*·kah	crazy
qilla	*ke*·lyah	lazy

qilqa	kel·kah	letter
qilqana	kel·kah·nah	pen • pencil
qilqay	kel·kai	to write
qincha	ken·chah	fence
qiru	ke·ro	cup (ceremonial, of the Incas)
qispi	kes·pee	crystal • glass • free (at liberty)
qulqisapa	kol·ke·sah·pah	rich
qunqay	kon·kai	to forget
qura	ko·rah	herb • plant
qurawan qampiq	ko·rah·wahn kahm·pekh	herbalist
quri	ko·ree	gold
qurpa	kor·pah	guest
qurpa wasi	kor·pah wah·see	accommodation
qurpachana	kor·pah·chah·nah	accommodation
quy	koy	to give • to pay
quya	ko·yah	queen
quykuy	koy·kui	to pay
quyllur	koy·lyoor	stars

QH

qhali kay	k-hah·lee kai	health
qhalilla	k-hah·lee·lyah	safe
qhampu	k-hahm·poo	spider
qhapaq	k-hah·pahkh	powerful • rich
qhapiru	k-hah·pee·roo	band
qhaqllin	k-hahkh·lyeen	jaw (lower)
qhari	k-hah·ree	man
qhatuy	k-hah·tui	to sell at a market
qhatu	k-hah·too	market
qhawachiy	k-hah·wah·chee	to show
qhawariy	k-hah·wah·ree	to look • to look after
qhaway	k-hah·wai	to watch • to see • care
qhilli	k-he·lyee	dirty
qhipapi	k-he·pah·pee	behind
qhipata	k-he·pah·tah	afterwards
qhipay	k-he·pai	to stay • to remain
qhusi	k-ho·see	blue (of eyes only)

Q'

q'aytu	k'ai·too	string
q'ipi	k'e·pee	backpack • package
q'ipiy	k'e·pee	to carry (on the back)
q'iyachay	k'e·yah·chai	to become infected
q'uchukuy	k'o·choo·kui	to celebrate

q'uncha	k'on·chah	stove
q'uñi	k'o·nyee	warm • hot
q'uñikuy	k'o·nyee·kui	to warm up
q'uñiy	k'o·nyee	to heat
q'upa	k'o·pah	garbage • rubbish
q'usmi	k'os·mee	smoke
q'usñi	k'os·nyee	smoke
q'uturichiy	k'o·too·ree·chee	to entertain

R

rakiy	rah·kee	to separate
rantiy	rahn·tee	to buy • to exchange • to barter
raphi	rah·p-hee	sheet (paper)
rap'a	rah·p'ah	page
raqch'i	rahkh·ch'ee	ceramic • pottery
raqra kunka	rahkh·rah koon·kah	hoarse
ratuchalla	rah·too·chah·lyah	fast (time)
ratulla	rah·too·lyah	quickly
rawray unquy	row·rai on·koy	temperature • fever
-rayku	·rai·koo	reason • because of
raymi	rai·mee	festival • holiday
rikch'akuq	reekh·ch'ah·kokh	lookalike • similar
rikch'aq	reekh·ch'ahkh	kind (type)
rikch'arichiy	reekh·ch'ah·ree·chee	to wake
rikch'ariy	reekh·ch'ah·ree	to wake
riki	ree·kee	of course
rikuchikuy	ree·koo·chee·kui	gift • present
rikurichiy	ree·koo·ree·chee	to exhibit
rikuy	ree·kui	to see
riluh	ree·lookh	clock • watch
rimay	ree·mai	to speak • to talk • language • word
rimaykuy	ree·mai·kui	to explain
ripuy	ree·pui	to leave • to go away
riqsichiy	rekh·see·chee	to show • to introduce (a person)
riqsinakuqmasi	rekh·see·nah·kokh·mah·see	friend
riqsisqa	rekh·sees·kah	famous
riqsiy	rekh·see	to know (people/places) • to get to know • to recognise
riy	ree	to go
rumi	roo·mee	rock • stone
runa	roo·nah	humankind • people • person • Quechua speaker

S

runakuna	roo·nah·*koo*·nah	people
rupha	*roo*·p·hah	fever • temperature • hot
ruphariy	roo·p·hah·ree	to feel hot (person)
ruphay	*roo*·p·hai	burn • sunlight
ruqya	*rokh*·yah	noise
ruq'tu	*rokh*'·too	deaf
ruruy	*roo*·rui	to produce
ruwana	roo·*wah*·nah	job
ruwanayuq	roo·wah·*nah*·yokh	busy
ruwasqa	roo·*wahs*·kah	done (a task)
ruway	*roo*·wai	to do • to make

S

saksasqa	sahkh·*sahs*·kah	full (after a meal)
saku	*sah*·koo	jacket (of a man)
samariy	sah·*mah*·ree	to breathe
samay	*sah*·mai	rest (relax) • to rest
sami	*sah*·mee	luck
samiyuq	sah·*mee*·yokh	lucky
sapa	*sah*·pah	alone • each • every
sapanka	sah·*pahn*·kah	each • every
sapaq	*sah*·pahkh	different • other
saqillay	sah·*ke*·lyai	to allow • to permit
saqiy	*sah*·kay	to leave something
saruy	*sah*·rui	to step on
sasa	*sah*·sah	hard • difficult
sat'iy	*sah*·t'ee	to inject • to puncture
sayachiy	sah·*yah*·chee	to stop (someone else)
sayaq	*sah*·yahkh	steep
sayarichiy	sah·yah·*ree*·chee	to build
sayay	*sah*·yai	to stop (oneself) • to stand • size • to size
sayk'usqa	sai·*k'oos*·kah	tired
saywa	*sai*·wah	border
sichus	*see*·choos	if
siki	*see*·kee	bottom (body)
silq'u	*sel*·k'o	signature
simi	*see*·mee	language • word • mouth • lip
sinchi	*seen*·chee	strong (person) • very
sipas	*see*·pahs	young woman
sipascha	see·*pahs*·chah	young woman
siq'inchay	se·*k'en*·chai	to draw
siqay	*se*·kai	to climb
siqsiy	*sekh*·see	itch (sensation)
siray	*see*·rai	to sew
sirikuy	*see*·*ree*·kui	to lie down

siriy	see·ree	to lie down
sispa	sees·pah	near • close
siwk	syookh	smooth • straight
sulpáy niy	sool·pai nee	to thank
sumaq	soo·mahkh	handsome • beautiful • nice • tasty
sumaq kawsayniyuq	soo·mahkh kow·sai·nee·yokh	honest
suni	soo·nee	long (length) • high
sunqu tupachiy	son·ko too·pah·chee	to (be in) love
suphu	soo·p·hoo	hair (body or animal)
suti	soo·tee	name
suti silq'uy	soo·tee sel·k'oy	to sign (a document)
sutichay	soo·tee·chai	to call • to name
sut'u	soo·t'oo	wet
suwakuy	soo·wah·kui	to rob
suway	soo·wai	to steal
suwirti	soo·weer·tee	luck
suyay	soo·yai	to expect • to wait
suyk'u	sui·k'oo	cup
suynay	sui·nai	sound
suyt'u	sui·t'oo	long (length) • high
suyu	soo·yoo	region

T

-ta	·tah	towards • to
taki	tah·kee	song
takiy	tah·kee	to sing
taksa	tahkh·sah	short • average
taksa puñuna	tahkh·sah poo·nyoo·nah	twin bed
takuriy	tah·koo·ree	to disturb
tanqay	tahn·kai	to push
tanta	tahn·tah	crowd • group
tapuna	tah·poo·nah	question
tapunakuy	tah·poo·nah·kui	to argue
tapuy	tah·pui	to ask (a question)
taqruy	tahkh·roy	to mix
tarikuy	tah·ree·kui	to find (something lost)
tarpuy	tahr·pui	to plant
tawa k'uchuyuq	tah·wah k'oo·choo·yokh	square (shape)
tayriyay	tai·ree·yai	to be late
timpuraq	teem·poo·rahkh	early in the afternoon
tinku	teen·koo	average • medium-sized
tinkuy	teen·kui	to meet • to meet up with
tiqsimuyu	tekh·see·moo·yoo	world • universe • space • time • Earth

tiyana	tee·*yah*·nah	chair • seat
tiyay	tee·yai	to live in • to sit
trawu	trah·woo	alcohol • liquor
trukiy	troo·kee	to barter • to exchange
tukay	too·kai	to play (music)
tukuy	too·kui	to finish • end • limit • everything • every • all
tullpa	tooly·pah	clay stove
tullu	too·lyoo	bone • thin • skinny
tupay	too·pai	to meet • to meet up with
tura	too·rah	friend (male friend of woman)
turi	too·ree	brother (of woman)
turiyay	too·ree·yai	to make fun of
tusuy	too·sui	dance • to dance
tuta	too·tah	evening • night • dark
tuta mikhuy	too·tah mee·k-hui	dinner
tutallamanta	too·tah·lyah·*mahn*·tah	early in the morning
tutamanta mikhuna	too·tah·*mahn*·tah mee·*k-hoo*·nah	breakfast
tutaraq	too·tah·rahkh	early in the morning
tutayay	too·*tah*·yai	to get dark
tuwalla	too·*wah*·lyah	towel

TH

thanta	t-han·tah	old (worn out)
thatkiy	t-haht·kee	to step

T'

t'aqasqa	t'ah·*kahs*·kah	separated
t'aqay	t'ah·kai	to separate
t'aqsay	t'ahkh·sai	to wash (clothes/hair)
t'ikray	t'eekh·rai	to translate
t'uqu	t'o·ko	hole • window
t'uru	t'oo·roo	mud

U

uhay	oo·hai	drink • to drink
uhu	oo·hoo	cough
uhuy	oo·hui	to cough
ukhu	oo·k-hoo	deep • inside
ukhupi	oo·*k-hoo*·pee	inside • among
ukyay	ookh·yai	drink • to drink
uliyay	oo·*lee*·yai	baptism

uma llaqta	oo·mah *lyahkh*·tah	capital city
unay	oo·nai	delay • to delay • past
upa	oo·pah	mute • deaf
uran	oo·rahn	below
uray	oo·rai	under
urmay	oor·mai	to fall
urpi	oor·pee	dove (also an endearment)
urpu	oor·poo	jar
usa	oo·sah	lice
usqhaq	oos·k-hahk	speedy
usqhay	oos·k-hai	fast • quickly (movement)
usqhaypaq	oos·k-hai·pahkh	urgent
usqhayta	os·k-hai·tah	immediately • very soon
ususi	oo·soo·see	daughter (of father)
utaq	oo·tahkh	or
uyakuy	oo·yah·kui	to agree to • to accept
uyariy	oo·yah·ree	to hear • to listen • to understand

W

wahay	wah·hai	to call (shout/ telephone)
wakcha	wahkh·chah	poor • poor person
wakcha kay	wahkh·chah kai	poverty
wakin	wah·keen	part • rest (remaining)
wakinkunalla	wah-keen·koo·*nah*·lyah	some (animate object)
wakiwakillan	wah·kee·wah·*kee*·lyan	some (inanimate object)
waksi	wahkh·see	steam
wampar	wahm·pahr	table
wampu	wahm·poo	boat
-wan	·wahn	with
wañusqa	wah·*nyoos*·kah	dead
wañuy	wah·nyui	to die
waq	wahkh	other
waqachiy	wah·*kah*·chee	to play (music)
waqay	wah·kai	to cry
waqaychay	wah·*kai*·chai	to keep
waqllichiy	wahkh·*lyee*·chee	to detour
waqlliy	wahkh·lyee	to detour
waqtanpi	wahkh·*tahn*·pee	beside (next to)
waqtu	wahkh·too	alcohol • liquor
waqyay	wahkh·yai	to call (shout/ telephone)
waq'a	wah·k'ah	crazy
wara	wah·rah	underpants • trousers

warmi	wahr·mee	wife • woman
warmichakuy	wahr·mee·chah·kui	to marry (man says)
wasi	wah·see	house
wasi ayllu	wah·see ai·lyoo	home
wasi-masi	wah·see·mah·see	neighbour
waskha	wahs·k·hah	rope
wata	wah·tah	year • age
wata hunt'ay	wah·tah hoon·t'ai	birthday
watay	wah·tai	to tie
watiqmanta	wah·tekh·mahn·tah	again
watukuy	wah·too·kui	to miss (person) • to visit
waturikuy	wah·too·ree·kui	to visit
watuq	wah·tokh	fortune teller
wat'a	wah·t'ah	island
wawa	wah·wah	baby (human)
wawa qhawaq	wah·wah k·hah·wahkh	babysitter
wawtisay	wow·tee·sai	baptism
wayaqa	wah·yah·kah	bag • purse • handbag
wayk'uy	wai·k'ui	to cook
wayllunakuy	wai·lyoo·nah·kui	to fall in love
waylluy	wai·lyui	love • to love
waylluq	wai·lokh	lover
wayna	wai·nah	young man
wayqi	wai·ke	brother (of man) • friend (male friend of man)
wayq'u	wai·k'o	deep valley
wayra	wai·rah	air
wayt'ay	wai·t'ai	to swim
wichay	wee·chai	to climb • up • uphill • north
wiksayuq	weekh·sah·yokh	pregnant (human)
willa	wee·lyah	news
willachikuy	wee·lyah·chee·kui	message
willakuy	wee·lyah·kui	to confess (tell) • story
willay	wee·lyai	to advise • to inform • to warn
wintana	ween·tah·nah	window
wiñay	wee·nyai	to grow • age
wiñay hunt'asqa	wee·nyai hoon·t'ahs·kah	adult
wira	wee·rah	fat • grease
wisikilita	wee·see·kee·lee·tah	bicycle
wisq'ana	wees·k'ah·nah	lock
wisq'asqa	wees·k'ahs·kah	shut
wisq'ay	wees·k'ai	to close • to shut
wulsiku	wool·see·koo	pocket
wutilla	woo·tee·lyah	bottle
wutilla kichana	woo·tee·lyah kee·chah·nah	bottle opener

Y

yachachiy	yah·*chah*·chee	to teach • to explain
yachay	yah·chai	to learn • to know (facts) • education
yachayniyuq	yah·chai·*nee*·yokh	intelligent • wise
yananchakuy	yah·nahn·*chah*·kui	to marry • wedding
yanapay	yah·*nah*·pai	to aid • to assist • to help
yanqallan	yahn·*kah*·lyahn	free (no cost)
yapamanta	yah·pah·*mahn*·tah	again
yapa yapa	*yah*·pah *yah*·pah	often
yaqa	*yah*·kah	almost • more or less
yawarchay	yah·*wahr*·chai	to bleed
yaya	*yah*·yah	priest • God
yunka	*yoon*·kah	jungle • forest
yupay	*yoo*·pai	to count
yupaychay	yoo·*pai*·chai	to respect • to worship
yupaychay wasi	yoo·*pai*·chai *wah*·see	temple
yuray	*yoo*·rai	to plant
yuyay	*yoo*·yai	to think • to remember • thought
yuyay quy	yoo·yai koy	advice
yuyariy	yoo·*yah*·ree	to remember
yuyaychay	yoo·*yai*·chai	to advise • to counsel
yuyaysapa	yoo·yai·*sah*·pah	intelligent • wise
yuyayukuy	yoo·yah·*yoo*·kui	to realise

INDEX

INDEX